Images of Light

Ascent to Trust in Triumph

SHARON R. CHACE

RESOURCE *Publications* · Eugene, Oregon

IMAGES OF LIGHT
Ascent to Trust in Triumph

Copyright © 2013 Sharon R. Chace. All rights reserved. Except for brief quotations in critical publications or reviews, no part of this book may be reproduced in any manner without prior written permission from the publisher. Write: Permissions, Wipf and Stock Publishers, 199 W. 8th Ave., Suite 3, Eugene, OR 97401.

Resource Publications
An Imprint of Wipf and Stock Publishers
199 W. 8th Ave., Suite 3
Eugene, OR 97401

www.wipfandstock.com

ISBN 13: 978-1-62032-475-2

Manufactured in the U.S.A.

New Revised Standard Version Bible, copyright © 1989, Division of Christian Education of the National Council of the Churches of Christ in the United States of America. Used by permission. All rights reserved.

Edna St. Vincent Millay, excerpts from "Never, before, perhaps, was such a sight," "Lapis and Sevres, and borage—every hue" and "I will control myself, or go inside." Copyright © 1951 by Norma Millay Ellis. Reprinted with the permission of The Permissions Company, Inc., on behalf of Holly Peppe, Literary Executor, The Millay Society, www.millay.org.

Ella's Gift: A Christmas Eve Story of Light is based on a previous version of the story published in the Town Times, a publication of The Record-Journal of Meriden, Connecticut and used by permission.

Dedicated to the members and friends
of the First Congregational Church
United Church of Christ
Rockport, Massachusetts

The Old Sloop by Sharon R. Parsons c. 1958

Contents

Acknowledgments   *ix*
Author's Note   *xi*
Introduction   *xix*

Birth

1   Light of a Star   3

     Nuit de Noel—Henri Matisse

2   Light of Inclusion   7

     Simeon's Song of Praise—Aert de Gelder

Teaching and Healing

3   Light of Forgiveness   13

     The Return of the Prodigal Son
     —Rembrandt van Rijn

4   Light of Caring   29

     The Good Samaritan (after Delacroix)
     —Vincent van Gogh

5   Light of Healing   41

     Tree of Life—Henri Matisse

Contents

Speaking Truth to Power

6   Light of Truth   53

Christ Before the High Priest
—Gerrit van Honthorst

Transfiguration and Resurrection

7   Light of the Transfiguration   59

Sailing Boats—Lyonel Feininger

The Glorious Victory of the Sloop "Maria"
—Lyonel Feininger

8   Light of the Resurrection   63

Resurrection—Matthias Grünewald

The Virgin and Child with St. George and St. Anthony Abbott—Antonio Pisanello

The Supper at Emmaus—Vincenzo Catena

Pietà (after Delacroix)—Vincent van Gogh

The Raising of Lazarus (after Rembrandt)
—Vincent van Gogh

Prayers   77

Conclusion as Contraries   81

Appendix:
Ella's Gift: A Christmas Eve Story of Light   83

Print Sources for Images   89

Bibliography   93

Acknowledgments

THANK YOU TO PEOPLE in communities of faith, scholarship, and art who I know personally and to countless people whom I have never met. People who believe in me or inspire me from the pages of religious and artistic heritage help make my artistic life possible. Both privilege and persistence actualize potential.

Thank you to the members of my class at First Congregational Church of Rockport for your presence, interest, and technological help. I am also grateful for professors over the years especially those who taught biblical studies and art. A look at the bibliography will make it clear that my favorite New Testament exegete is Fr. Daniel J. Harrington, SJ of the School of Theology and Ministry at Boston College. My undergraduate professor, John L. Cheek, gave me a strong foundation in historical criticism and appreciation for biblical sources that support the social gospel.

I remember with gratitude studio art courses and art history courses at Albion College in Albion, Michigan. Professors Vernon L. Bobbitt, Constance Fowler, Richard Leach, and Paul Stewart all saw beyond my fragility and fatigue to glimpse future possibility. Artists over the centuries, who have struggled with what it means to be both religious and painterly, are deeply appreciated. Dr. Kathleen Powers Erickson read the manuscript and offered helpful comments especially about Vincent van Gogh. The folks at Wipf and Stock publishers, especially Christian Amondson,

Acknowledgments

Patrick Harrison, and Christopher Layton, were helpful with their editorial and artistic expertise.

Through his weekly exegetical comments the Rev. Harry T. Cook, who did his undergraduate work at Albion College, helps me in my goal to be bridge-building and willing to wrestle with New Testament Greek. At a college reunion around 1986 I reconnected with Robina Quale-Leach who taught history with emphasis on intellectual history. She has given on-going encouragement. Like her late husband Richard Leach, whom she married late in life after Professor Leach lost his beloved first wife, Robina discerned my strengths and helped me bloom. Friend Sarah Clark, who is a retired Unitarian Universalist minister, read a very early version of my manuscript. Her interest gave me courage to proceed. Sarah has shown up at my house with her dog Nellie at the exact moments when I have most needed her advice.

Librarian Camilla Ayers works hard on interlibrary loans for me and for other library patrons. I am thankful to her and to the Brandeis Library for their generous loan of *The Healing Presence of Art: A History Of Western Art in Hospitals* when this extraordinary book was hot off the press.

My husband Ernest took the photograph of the John Avery mural. He and daughter Amy Elizabeth are my two best cheerleaders. I thank them for their enthusiasm.

Author's Note

WHEN REV. JAMES FLETCHER, who was Interim Pastor of the First Congregational Church in Rockport, Massachusetts, asked me to design what was originally planned as an Advent program, I did not think that I could do it. My muscles were tense. My mind was tepid. I had thoughts and tentative outlines but my heart was not upbeat.

After a few anxious nights, a dream that took me two days to understand set my mind on fire. Focus was a gift from God working through my subconscious. In this dream I was in our church in Rockport and had trouble visually focusing on the hymn printed on golden-yellow paper as a bulletin insert. No idea what hymn! However the golden-yellow showed up in many images that I selected for this course. One woman, who took my course on which this book is based, asked if I chose the pictures because of the golden yellow. No. I selected the paintings because of the light that I saw in them. I did not notice the yellow-gold in the images until well into the writing of this book. Happiness of yellow is a thread woven through these essays.

Finally in my dream I could clearly see the words on the last verse. Then the cross over the altar disappeared. In its place there was a recessed window with a view of Mt. Monadnock in New Hampshire. The mountain was back-lit in a luminous, light blue, and bathed in green and coral. Mountain images have always been important to me. Mountains in the east and in the west readily evoke Psalm

Author's Note

121. In the first two verses the Psalmist asks where his help comes from and then answers his own question by concluding that his help comes from the Lord who is the maker of heaven and earth.

> "I lift up my eyes to the hills—
> from where will my help come?
> My help comes from the Lord,
> who made heaven and earth." Ps 121:1–2

This psalm is a song of trust.[1] It is also a psalm of ascent in a group of fifteen ascent psalms (120–134). The psalmist proclaims confidence in God's continual care through night and day. Pilgrims on their way, ascending the hills to Jerusalem and to the Temple, trusted these words of assurance that they would not be done in by robbers. These robbers were like those who tortured the man found by the Good Samaritan in Luke's gospel. In this psalm God the Keeper and the Good Samaritan are kin. Therefore there is an especially bright spark of divine love in people who are good Samaritans. People can be good Samaritans offering company and protection to one another on the ascent to trust in the triumph of good over evil.

The theme of life as a mountainous journey is deep in the Puritan soul ever since John Bunyan wrote his classic The Pilgrim's Progress, which is an undercurrent in the flow of this book. There are many hills to climb in a lifetime. The ascent to trust is only one trek, yet it underlies all quests. Trust is a multi-faceted diamond of faith in God, self-assurance, confidence in trustworthy neighbors and belief in human possibilities for goodness. You, my readers, have your own private dreams and mountains. Like Bunyan you can trust in "shoes and prayers" on your ascent to trust in transcendent goodness and to your personal goal. When

---

1. Harrington, *Why Do We Hope?* 83–84.

Author's Note

people love God and care about others, personal goals are woven into hope for the ultimate triumph of the reign of love and light.

Journey to the Sun

When stars seem
out of reach, it is time
to consider feet.
Claim the symbol of
keeping on trudging and
meter-measure of
striving and trying.
Revisit the Puritan past.
Join the Pilgrim on
his progress and trust
in "shoes and prayers."

The Advent program had to be cancelled, which turned out to be a blessing. Expanding the material birthed a book that people can use anytime. As poets do I turned weeks of prose writing into a short poem that is a summary of the core belief in this course. Whether we wait for the coming of the baby Jesus during Advent or for Easter joy during Lent, the promise that light will win over against darkness is a constant blessing. Nature underscores human yearnings for light. In the dark days of Advent we cherish light. In the lengthening days of Lent we wait for the days of longest light. Advent waiting can also be Easter waiting. The Christmas tree can be understood as a tree of life.

Advent Waiting

Sunlight shining through scallop shells
glowing on the Christmas tree
creates symbols of sacred journeys

Author's Note

> to Wisdom's winning light.
> Glowing on the Christmas tree
> each ornament hung with hope to turn
> to Wisdom's winning light
> when darkness will be overcome by goodness.
>
> Each ornament hung with hope to turn
> creates symbols of sacred journeys
> when darkness will be overcome by goodness.
> Sunlight shining through scallop shells.

The main idea of this book is: Contemplating artistic and biblical images of light can help people navigate life as they ascend to trust in the triumph. The victory is human goodness that is informed by Jesus and other wise people. The climb to the mountain top of trust is a spiritual adventure. The summit may be Bethlehem, Jerusalem, Easter or your own individual high point of personal triumph. The symbol of mountains as the destination on life's journey is broader than the cross. Nor does every journey, even a Christian pilgrimage, mean martyrdom of the cross. As you know from reading the Bible, martyrdom that seems certain in the Gospel of Mark changes into day by day sacrificial living in the Gospel of Luke. Your adventure may take place in Advent, a word, which is tied to adventure, or at any other time. Whether you are a theist or a humanist, one way to prepare for Christ's light coming during any season of the year, for Christ does not come just at Christmas, is to consider the implicit meaning of both Christmas and Easter in the prologue of the Gospel of John (1:1–5). The gospel writer concludes with a declarative sentence of promise. "The light shines in the darkness, and the darkness did not overcome it."

The prologue is so significant that I quote the whole passage.

Author's Note

In the beginning was the Word, and the Word was with God, and the Word was God. He was in the beginning with God. All things came into being through him, and without him not one thing came into being. What has come into being in him was life, and the life was the light of all people. The light shines in the darkness, and the darkness did not overcome it. (John 1:1–5)

When Jesus grows up, the infant Jesus of Matthew's and Luke's gospels will lift his followers by the winning light of his wisdom. In Matthew, Jesus will preach from a mountain about light and love of neighbor, rest and challenge, forgiveness and fairness. In Luke's gospel, Jesus' teachings are more fully developed in stories. As we ponder pictorial images that depict different meanings of light, you will discover your ways of keeping light burning so brightly that the light that is yours will help goodness triumph. Unless, for example, you are talking about a light bulb, light is an abstract noun. In order to make light more concrete it is necessary to speak about the light of something more tangible. I have done so by writing about the light of a star, the light of inclusion, the light of forgiveness, the light of caring, the light of healing, the light of speaking truth to power, the light of the transfiguration, and the light of resurrection. Finding or reaffirming your ways of participating in Christ's light is an on-going exploration of your spirituality. Living in the light is a way to participate in God-like healing love. Being lights in the world can help one another sustain trust in the implicit meaning of Christmas and Easter that darkness will not overcome light.

Paths to embracing the wise teachings of Jesus, the Light of the World, will not all be alike. Still there are common experiences of welcome and inclusion, forgiveness and acceptance, speaking up for others and caring for individuals, healing and rest. Christ's light can lift people of faith in God or in humanity to the wonders of his loving wisdom.

Author's Note

When inclusion and forgiveness, which artists help us to see, are realized there is a taste of God's reign in the present and a glimpse of future fullness of goodness of God's reign or Eden restored. Informed by a Wounded Innocence: Sketches for a Theology of Art by Alejando Garcia-Rivera, Cecilia González-Andrieu wrote: "The Christian tradition affirms that Jesus Christ teaches us how to be fully human. The beautiful in art can move our heart at its depths, bringing us to a state in which we are open to seeing Christ and imagining the reign of God he came to usher in. Aesthetics is about hope and the 'theological dimension of art lies in that, ultimately, art interprets humanity to the human.'"[2] Insight into the human condition and even into God, to my mind, is the most fruitful function of art.

The flow of the chapters in this book reflects the life of Jesus from birth through ministry of teaching, healing, speaking truth to power, and onto transfiguration and resurrection. While affirming the historicity of Jesus, he is also a mythic hero because his life journey has much in common with all humanity. Birth, life, and death are markers on all human journeys. As mythic hero Jesus the Christ shines through the earthly triumph of being true to his calling and the ongoing triumph of his teachings that continue in the lives of his followers. However you understand resurrection it is triumphant goodness. When anyone persists and climbs the arduous and good mountain of one's choosing, there is a heroic moment of triumph.

In the Lenten course on which this book is based, I selected four kinds of spiritual light for a four week course. After my short presentations that included pictures from art history, there was time for answering questions as well as for sharing thoughts and feelings.

---

2. González-Andrieu, *Bridge to Wonder*, 56.

Author's Note

As you know, images are expensive to publish so I have used only a few. However there is a list of the images and the books in which you can find them in the appendix.

Thank you, my readers, for your reading and for your seeing.

Grace and Peace,
Sharon

Introduction

Looking at Art

THERE IS NO ONE correct way to look at art. This essay is intended as a guide for your consideration. Because this book focuses on meanings, it makes sense to start by thinking about art as disclosure. In his book *A Theological Approach to Art*, the late Roger Hazelton discussed art as disclosure. He said that often artists do not want to talk about their work. Being an artist I concur. Sometimes I want to talk about my paintings and at other times I do not. Yet years ago I put aside the sixties notion that art must stand on its own with the mantra: "Either people get it or they do not." Likewise Hazelton said that we need all the clues we can get! Picasso said that "Art is a lie that makes us realize the truth."[1] Hazelton admits that lie may be an exaggeration but in his thought, that I am simplifying, imaginary images can speak to us as real. Therefore art can be disclosure. Revelation is an unveiling of human meaning.

Drawing upon the thought of a Swiss writer and cultural historian, Denis de Rougemont, Hazelton characterizes art as a trap for meditation that is understood as pause and focus.[2] Meaning is disclosed in its rich complexity and opens dialogue. (I wish Hazelton offered the word

1. Hazelton, *A Theological Approach to Art*, 16.
2. Ibid., 21.

Looking at Art

"invitation" as an alternative to the word "trap.") In either case truth comes in the context of a rich "community of meaning." To slightly paraphrase Hazelton, there may be an encounter with truth, as for example, in the form of compassionate identification, as so often is felt when viewing Rembrandt.[3]

In her book, *Bridge to Wonder: Art as a Gospel of Beauty,* Cecilia González-Andrieu, also considers art as disclosure. She claims that the possibility of disclosure of meaning(s) is a nonnegotiable principle for the interlacing of art and religion. To summarize her thought; meaning in theological aesthetics may be thought of as insight. Prompting insight can be seen as converging in experiences of art and experiences of revelation.[4] Put very simply in my words: Look at a painting and enjoy the beauty of joy and celebration or the incongruous prophetic beauty of suffering and pain. Enjoy loveliness in the world. Embrace your own pain or the suffering of others. Through seeing you may receive fresh revelation of meanings, insight about yourself, understandings of the human condition or even inner visions of the face of God.

Receiving the Message

Art cannot be unpacked like unpacking the message in linear prose. I propose five features of interpretation.

1. Acknowledgement that once the painting has left the artist's hands it is open to interpretation. Therefore meanings are polyvalent or to put it more simply paintings may have many meanings. To reiterate Hazelton, there can be rich complexity and communities

3. Ibid, 34.
4. González-Andrieu, *Bridge to Wonder*, 115.

of meanings. Therefore discussion groups may open up new insights and multiple interpretations that are not mutually exclusive.

2. Unless you have primary sources such as letters by the artist that tell what he or she intended as meanings, we cannot know for certain what the artist meant.

3. Understanding art as artistic metaphor rather than literal is an important interpretive lens. Artistic metaphors are not likely to be in dispute. I have never heard anyone insist that his or her favorite artists painted angels exactly as they looked on the first Noel! Metaphors suggest connotations. Cherub angels who are not old enough to talk may connote joy and happiness but not singing. Angels of an adult age can suggest singing angels. Understood metaphorically angels are likely to be seen as literary or artistic devices to convey joy, or celebration, religious significance, or spiritual presence.

Symbols are related to metaphors but are not exactly the same. Symbol defined very broadly or personally can be close to metaphor as, for example, seeing a dragonfly as a symbol of life. Symbols stand for something and in the thought of Paul Tillich participate in the reality to which they point. Hence a flag participates in the dignity of a nation.[5] In a different line of thought that stresses visual rather than just verbal ways of knowing, González-Andrieu throughout her book shows the power of symbols in art to be revelatory. Metaphors connote a likeness described in words or images. A metaphor gives a likeness without using the word "like" as does a simile.

---

5. Tillich, *Dynamics of Faith*, 42.

The original meaning of the word *rock* is a stone or boulder. Using the word metaphorically to connote strength or reliability you might say: My best friend is a rock. A symbol can be used metaphorically as when someone says she or he has a heavy cross to bear. As a symbol a cross stands for Christianity or crucifixion or suffering and participates in the reality of suffering. As metaphor it connotes general suffering.

Symbols and metaphors may be more easily found in language, especially poetry. However, language is not everything. When you perceive symbolic or metaphorical meanings in art, take your sightings seriously. Those symbols, whether explicit or implicit may be revelatory or in some way mediate God or the best in humanity.

4. Describing the subject matter and if possible noting the historical context of a painting anchors the image in time and guards against interpretations that are too far-fetched.

5. Consideration of artistic elements such as color, light, form, perspective, and contrasts in dark and light helps disclose meanings. Personal experiences of color and light may affect interpretation.

My personal story about blue may resonate. My first experience of revelatory beauty occurred when I was three years old. My mother Katharine Rogers Parsons was dying of leukemia. Light filtered through cobalt blue vases on the windowsill and gave me comfort. Mother was very ill yet she found time to color with me. My favorite color was blue.

Beauty mattered and settled within. Color was a visual parable of grace. Are vases art? (Maybe not,

Introduction: Looking at Art

maybe yes) In any case, color is one of the formal art elements that artists use. When pictorial images are not present, color alone can speak.

The importance of truth dawned in my impressionable mind. Following the conventional wisdom of the time, my father did not want anyone to talk with me about death. The only person who did was the minister who visited the playgroup at the Universalist Church in Gloucester, Massachusetts. Although I do not remember the exact conversation, I do remember building with blocks as we talked. Unlike beauty and truth, which are eternal, my play structures toppled. When truth and beauty are important, an interest in theological aesthetics may follow.

Forty-five years after my mother died, I created a watercolor collage that depicts God's dwelling as blue. This image is based on Exodus 24:9–10 where the elders of Israel go up a mountain and see under God's feet something like a pavement of sapphire stones like the very heaven for clearness. The word *like* suggests a poetic and visual simile for "very heaven." Russian blue is the purest blue I have ever found. Even cobalt blue seems a tinge muddy in comparison. I painted Russian and other shades of blue through tissue paper and then pasted pieces of paper onto heavier watercolor paper. God is not a red dot. But God is a focal point as is the splotch of red in my picture. Taking poetic license and using the word *Fathers* in honor of our parental forerunners instead of the more technically correct term *Elders* I also wrote a poem. Once again I saw God in the color blue.

Looking at Art

Blue Sonnet

> Blue morning glories reach from ground to sky,
> Jacob's ladder connecting earth, heaven.
> Singing, angel muse patiently stands by.
> Pure hue, glory, loveliness is leaven.
> Hagar looking upon the face of God
> Lived. So shall those whose gaze is strong enough
> To embrace the icon nourished in sod.
> Beauty so deep sadness is joyful hush.
> Fathers of Israel saw beneath God's feet
> A sapphire pavement. Hallow, praise, chant.
> Sing in Heaven's City evil's defeat.
> Foundations of treasured, precious blue stone,
> Power, purest presence, God's face alone.

A Process for Interpreting Your Own Favorite Picture

You may come across images that appeal to you. If you wish, consider the general guidelines and expanded commentary below and write your own thought.

1. Describe the subject matter and if possible mention the historical context.
2. Why are you attracted to this picture?
3. Think about the colors, light, and other artistic elements and how they affect your feelings and understandings of the picture. How do these elements contribute to the meaning? Have you had an experience of color that affects your discovery of meaning?
4. Do you identify with the subject matter or people in a scene?

Introduction: Looking at Art

5. Asking what the picture means to you is an important question yet is often best asked after considering the subject matter, artistic elements, and historical background.
6. When considering what a painting means to you ask yourself if you see a valued aspect of yourself in a painting or if the image offers you comfort or consolation or even compensation.
7. Are there any images in the painting that to you become symbolic? If so, what does the symbol(s) reveal to you?

Counterpoint and Expanded Commentary

Take what I just wrote in point 5 about the importance of historical background with caution. This expanded commentary will help you make more sense of point 6. Of course if you try to make a case about the painter's intended message you need background and primary sources such as letters written by the artist. However for this course we will follow Margaret R. Mile's distinction between the message given and the message received[6] or in my phrasing the message intended and the message interpreted. You never know when an image will reach out and grab you and you need to explore your reactions right away before you can get to books of art history.

To reiterate Hazelton art discloses meanings. Years later Margaret Miles provided guidance about finding personally significant images and contemplating them. In her chapter "Language and Images: A Theory" in her book, *Image as Insight: Visual Understanding in Western Christianity*

---

6. Miles, *Image as Insight: Visual Understanding in Western Christianity and Secular Culture*, 28.

Looking at Art

and Secular Culture, Miles suggests ways to find images that speak to us. She advises looking at a variety of images including ones we see every day and those we seek out. We must gather those images that engage us and place them where we can see them in various moods and situations. Miles' observations and my thoughts converge. As I note in my forthcoming discussion of the light of inclusion, I understand the painting *Simeon's Song of Praise* differently at different times.

Miles says that the images we select will fall into basically two types. These types are: 1) Expression of a valued aspect of our experience, and 2) Compensation or alternative to our individual experience. Miles wrote: "The dark-skinned Madonna on my wall does not express, but it visually compensates, the pace of my day."[7] In summary she says that we need images to express or help us see what we are about and we need images to represent or make present some aspects of human possibility that we have known, perhaps momentarily. As we progress through this course we will keep in mind art as expressing glimpses of a valued aspect of our experiences and art as compensation, comfort, or consolation. As pointed out during a class based on this course book, there are alternative words to compensation such as comforting or consoling. My sense is that the words *comfort* and *consolation* are broader and are lesser claims. These three words, *compensation, comfort*, and *consolation*, are not chemically pure, nor mutually exclusive. I will use all of them.

Miles points out that the images that strike us can be a painting in a museum of a soup can. A sentence she wrote crediting Albert Camus stops me with the force of recognition. "A line, a color, may be enough to touch us; we will contemplate that line, that color, until we recognize in it,

7. Ibid., 149.

Introduction: Looking at Art

perhaps, the perfect mother none of us has ever known, the stimulating or comforting touch for which we long when we feel 'the mortal cold of the universe.'"[8]

Because the dark-skinned Madonna is a significant image for Miles one wonders what personal experiences inform that sentence. I am also reminded of a story in a collection of stories that I collected in the eighties. I discovered my historical friend Jane Holmes in a Harvard Divinity School course, "Women Speaking in the American Protestant Traditions," taught by Dr. Phyllis Blum Cole. My observation was that her whole spirituality evolved around the death of her mother. After the course, I collected stories of adult women who as young girls lost their mothers in death as I had. Dr. Myra Reid Grant found comforting images in the paintings of Mary Cassatt. Images of mothers and children can take on symbolic meanings. Bonds of mother love and eternal inclusion are implicit promises in Cassatt's work. Discovering personal symbols sustains the finders. Art can be revelatory.

I did not know about Mary Cassatt's paintings until I was in college. At that time I valued her mother and child images. My embrace of her work may have been foreshadowed. In retrospect at age 12, I found an organic image of mother love in the hen and chickens plants in our backyard. No wonder I made a red hen surrounded by yellow chickens in a seventh grade pottery class. As an adult, a biblical feminine image of God as a mother hen in Matthew 23:37 resonates.

When we explore art, biblical text, and contemporary stories about the Prodigal Son, you will see how Henri Nouwen found compensating images for a sense of being at home and loved through Rembrandt's art. In his case I sense that the word *compensating* is not too strong because

8. Ibid.

Looking at Art

Nouwen seemed to lack acceptance or knew it only fleetingly. At the same time, *comforting* and *consoling* also are fitting and offer the richness of nuances. To reiterate: Ask yourself if you see a valued aspect of your experience in a painting or if the image offers you comfort, consolation, or even compensation.

In summary: Once art has left the artist's hands, it is open to interpretation. Art can disclose meanings. Art may reflect our experiences or offer alternative experiences. There will be multiple interpretations of pictorial images and a diversity of meanings.

Birth

Matthew 2

1

Light of a Star

Marquette for Nuit de Noel
Henri Matisse
1952
123 1/8 by 53 1/2 in
Collection, Museum of Modern Art, New York.
Gift of Time, Inc.

NOT ONLY IS THE *Light of a Star* a chapter title, it is a charter granting courage to hope. Guided by the Star of Bethlehem the Wise Men hoped to find the King of the Jews. When they found the baby Jesus, I wonder if those intelligent visitors intuitively knew that like them the holy infant would grow up to be wise.

Wisdom is cosmopolitan. People of different centuries and cultures possess it. While the New Testament locates Divine Wisdom in Jesus, or put another way, portrays Jesus as the Word, there is a quiet hint that wisdom was divinely present at creation before the earthly life of the historical Jesus.

Images of Light

"In the beginning was the Word, and the Word was with God, and the Word was God. He was in the beginning with God. All things came into being through him, and without him not one thing came into being. What has come into being in him was life, and the life was the light of all people. The light shines in the darkness, and the darkness did not overcome it" (John 1:1–5).

Because God's word that called forth light came before creation of humanity and the writing of the Bible, wisdom is even older than the Bible. Yet biblical writers help readers understand wisdom at large in the universe. The Old Testament book of Proverbs affirms God's creation of a slightly personalized wisdom in the beginning of the cosmos (8:22). Word in the prologue of John's Gospel links the human mind to the mind of God because God and people can think. *Logos* or the New Testament Greek word for Word is not simply a spoken word such as God's word at creation in Genesis 1 but in Greek thought the divine principle of reason that gives order to the universe.[1] This word connotes reason, sense, meaning, and idea.[2] Because people can reason and be wise, all of humanity is linked with the mind of God.

Shining in the night sky over a stable and the whole world, the star is a symbol for hope in God or for hope in transcendent good will whether divine or human in origin. You can imagine light shining through the stained glass windows that were based on this paper version of *Nuit de Noel*. In his *Nuit de Noel*, Matisse used white to create light and colored shapes to suggest spiritual space. Organic shapes mold his vision of a Christmas Eve sky. Sea and earth and sky are connected by blue blocks, which lift the viewer's eyes from the deepest ocean to the highest heaven.

1. *The Harper Collins Study Bible*, 2013.
2. Swenson, *Bible Babel*, 122.

Light of a Star

Hope lifts the human heart to transcendent possibilities for self and society.

Christians yearn to participate in the life of God. People of many faiths and humanists hope for a better world. Wisdom is for sharing. It is important to note the universal presence of wisdom because our American society can no longer be described in the words of Will Herberg as "Catholic, Protestant, and Jew." Margaret R. Miles, historical and intellectual historian, raised a very important question in her lecture, "Short Beds and Narrow Sheets: Religion and the Common Good": "Is it possible to be passionately committed to one's religion while remaining humble about universal truth claims?"[3] Harry T. Cook wrote, "Imagine the relaxation of tension and conflict in the world if only religious leaders of the various communities of faith were to refrain from claiming absolute and exclusive truth for their sacred texts."[4] Further thoughts that Cook offered more fully addresses Miles' question by suggesting a perspective that could help one be committed to his or her beliefs and at the same time remain humble. Writing about world peace, in his emailed essay, *It Would Be One Giant Leap for Mankind,* July 7, 2012, he said, "A breakthrough could come were respected scholars of Hinduism, Judaism, Christianity and Islam to acknowledge that their individual belief systems are, at best, metaphoric approximations of what may be true."[5] One does not need to be a scholar to be bridge-building to people of different faiths by considering one's own beliefs to be metaphorical approximations of what could be true. Openness could be a window to let in the light of wisdom.

3. Miles, "Short Beds and Narrow Sheets: Religion and the Common Good," video.

4. Cook, *Long Live Salvation by Works*, 102.

5. Harry Cook, email message to the author, July 7, 2012.

Images of Light

In a world brightened by sunlight by day and starlight by night, people search for common ground and common good. Inclusion trumps exclusivity. Forgiveness wins. Caring is triumphant. Sickness gives way to healing. Light is born anew.

QUESTIONS FOR DISCUSSION

1. What are your general or specific hopes for yourself?
2. What are your general or specific hopes for the world?
3. Do you envision a time when people of different faiths will work together for the common good?
4. Is working together for the common good already happening on Cape Ann or where you live?

Luke 2

2

Light of Inclusion

Simeon's Song of Praise
Aert de Gelder
c.1700
oil on canvas
37 by 43 in
Mauritshuis Museum, The Hague

REMBRANDT TAUGHT HIS PUPIL, Aert de Gelder, how to paint light. He painted a scene of light shining in inclusive love. In Aert de Gelder's painting, *Simeon's Song of Praise*, the old Hebrew priest receives the infant Jesus for his dedication service of circumcision. Wrapped warmly in his snuggle blanket, baby Jesus is immersed in loving light. With her hands folded in prayer the woman facing Jesus has often been seen as Anna who worshipped continually in the Temple. So certain have people been that the woman is Anna, sometimes the painting has been titled *Simeon and Anna Pray to baby Jesus*.

Images of Light

However, Sister Wendy sees the woman as Mary.[1] As I have said before, art is open to interpretation. If there is only one angle, especially if it is dogmatic or didactic, art is in danger of being propaganda which de Gelder's art is most certainly not. Although I want the prayerful woman to be Anna in honor of Anna's prayer life and in regard to some traditions, I also believe for two reasons that the woman is Mary. Firstly, Anna in Luke's story about Simeon's enlightenment when Mary and Joseph brought Jesus to the temple is eighty-four years old. The woman I see as Mary most of the time appears much younger. (However, different sources of light in our home affect how I see this painting.) Simeon also looks younger but not that much younger. In my imagination perhaps some days the woman will be Anna and at other times she will be Mary.

Secondly, in the background a male figure, who blends into the warm darkness, may be Joseph, there with his wife Mary, but as in the New Testament overshadowed by her. Rev. Jim suggested the possibility that the man in the background might symbolize a stranger who was welcomed and included.

Whoever the people are, Simeon and Jesus are the visual center and main concern. Visually the red blanket is the focal point that thrusts the eyes upward to Simeon's face filled with wonder, amazement, and the peace of realizing his deepest desire to see universal salvation for Jews and Gentiles alike. Rev. Jim preached on this passage and adult daughter Amy asked me how Simeon knew that the baby Jesus was the Messiah. Intuition is possible. The Holy Spirit, which can inspire through intuition, is important in Luke's writings. It is also possible that Luke created the story to explain his understanding of inclusion and chose to express his views in historical fiction. Amy then wondered

1. Beckett, *Sister Wendy's 1000 Masterpieces*, 165.

if some people knew that Jesus was the Messiah through his preaching. Well, preaching can be very persuasive. If people were clued in by the Holy Spirit or their own thoughtful assessments before Jesus began to preach, his preaching must have added convincing data.

In his adult life Jesus will experience misunderstanding and rejection, yet in Simeon's adoring presence he is off to a good start with a foundation of love, a font of blessings. So also are our children off to a good start at Baptism, welcoming them into faith communities of inclusion and commitment to social justice. The love that Jesus received as an infant must have helped him forge his ethics of forgiveness and love of neighbor. So those baptized with water and those dedicated to loving service will have the potential to grow in wisdom and in loving concern.

Luke's gospel fills out the details of de Gelder's painting and the painting in turn secures the sacred power inherent in this story of inclusive love. In Luke's story (2:21–40), which reveals Jesus as a "light for revelation" to the Gentiles and foreshadows his life, Simeon is a devout man looking forward to the consolation of Israel. He knew through the Holy Spirit that he would not die before he had seen the Lord's Christ. Taking Jesus in his arms, he praised God saying:

> "Master, now you are dismissing
> your servant in peace,
> according to your word;
> for my eyes have seen your salvation,
> which you have prepared in the
> presence of all peoples,
> a light for revelation to the Gentiles
> and for glory to your people Israel." (29–32)

Images of Light

Jesus as light for the Gentiles and for the glory of Israel is an image of inclusion. The birth of inclusion is holy birth. There is sacred power in inclusive love that creates communities of caring that heal the brokenhearted. The light of inclusion lifts us as individuals and as faith communities beyond ourselves to heights of trust in triumph.

Questions for Discussion

1. Do you believe that Luke's story or de Gelder's painting confirm a biblical foundation for your efforts to make people feel welcomed in your church?
2. When have you felt either excluded or included?
3. How does inclusion light the world?
4. Does this painting suggest something of significance to you, or express an alternative experience?
5. Does this painting offer you any kind of compensation or consolation?

Teaching and Healing

Luke 15

3

Light of Forgiveness

The Return of the Prodigal Son
Rembrandt van Rijn
1668–69
Oil on Canvas
80.7 by 103.1 in
Hermitage Museum

LOOKING AT REMBRANDT'S PAINTING *The Return of the Prodigal Son* can be thoughtful and prayerful. Putting your thoughts into words is an offering of heart, mind, and soul. Identification with one or more characters in the story will help you understand yourself and also your relationships to other people and to God, in whatever way you know or imagine him or her.

Rembrandt was a keen observer of human nature. One humorous example of Rembrandt's perception is seen in his drawing around 1635 entitled *The Naughty Boy*. A frustrated mother unsuccessfully tries to restrain her squirmy, slippery, angry child who is yelling and throwing a toy.[1]

1. Durham, *The Biblical Rembrandt*, 28.

Images of Light

Siblings trail behind the mother. An older woman bends over to look at the child with an expression that conveys both concern and criticism. She could be a grandmother or mother-in-law. In my imagination based on experience I hear an elderly member of the church council saying, "Enjoy them while they are young!" True enough, but not what a young mother wants to hear at the time of the tantrum!

Throughout Rembrandt's life he grew in understanding of biblical stories and how biblical passages applied to him. "The Bible was, for Rembrandt, a sourcebook and a mirror of the human situation, a vision of what might have been, and of what might be, and so at last a sourcebook of faith. Not an orthodox faith, by any measure of orthodoxy—but then, can real faith, faith at its most personal, ever really be orthodox?"[2] Rembrandt painted a number of pictures with old women reading heavy books that appear to be bibles. By popular tradition they are linked to Rembrandt's mother.[3] Of course in a Dutch Reform culture, the Bible was a constant presence. John I. Durham, who taught biblical languages and Old Testament theology immersed himself in looking, pondering, and dialoguing with Rembrandt for well over forty years wrote: "I think Rembrandt came to the Bible without pretense, read it without the pious blinders religious people so often wear, and accepted it as a word from God, in no need of any human attempt to turn it into a talisman, an answer book, or a rabbit's left hind foot. Thus did the Bible speak to Rembrandt, and thus does the Bible speak through Rembrandt."[4] In Durham's estimation he appears to have begun his biblical works with

2. Ibid., 2.
3. Ibid., 53.
4. Ibid., 234.

Light of Forgiveness

the biblical text. Then he lived with those texts, internalized them and saw people he knew and his own life in them.[5]

To my mind the most moving glimpses of Rembrandt's style of response to scripture that Durham gives his readers are the accounts of Rembrandt's inclusion of himself in his work. Durham does not mention St. Ignatius of Loyola but this saint comes to my mind immediately because the first class that I took at Weston Jesuit School of Theology was *The Theological and Pastoral Dimensions of the Spiritual Exercises of St. Ignatius Loyola.* For me this course gave me the needed motivation and direction to continue my studies and in time the discernment to know that my best way to serve Christ is through writing. In this class we experienced a modified form of the *Spiritual Exercises*. As individuals we imagined the place and details of a biblical scene about which we prayed. For example, one question we might have prayerfully pondered while picturing a crucifixion scene is how do we contribute to the crucifixion of Christ? It seems to me that a similar process must have informed Rembrandt.

While I cherish my poetic connection between Rembrandt and Ignatius, I doubt that Ignatius was a household word in the van Rijn family. Even though Rembrandt's mother was Catholic, his parents must have remembered the hostilities between Spain and the Protestant United Providences.

Sometime in 1625 Rembrandt painted his earliest known painting, *Stoning of Stephen*. This painting is based on Acts 7:58 in which the crowd stones Stephen to death. What is most remarkable is that "peering out at us from a position just above and behind Stephen's head is Rembrandt himself—a bit of confession perhaps, a statement at least, and of a kind Rembrandt made across at least twenty-five

5. Ibid., 59.

15

years."⁶ Is it not possible that by placing himself in the scene Rembrandt considered how he might hurt the saint?

In *Christ Preaching* (The Hundred Guilder Print, 1640–1650), which includes many sick or confrontational people in chapter 19 of Matthew, Rembrandt is in the crowd between Jesus and his critics, with Peter reaching out his hand to restrain a woman coming forward with her baby.⁷ Yet as you know from your reading of the New Testament, Jesus said not to send the children away because they belong to the Kingdom of heaven. Durham wonders if Rembrandt was asking himself what he would have done if he had been there.⁸

Rembrandt wearing a blue-green beret shows up in his painting of the crucifixion, *The Raising of the Cross*. Durham believes that what moves this painting from a biblical moment to a statement of meaning is a statement of Rembrandt's own involvement in an event that he contemplated throughout his life. He did not want to be there and painted himself in a moment of regret with the resolve to do better.⁹ In like manner in *The Descent from the Cross,* Rembrandt's face is one of pain and regret¹⁰ as he helps remove Christ's body for burial. Such immersion and identification with place and characters is consistent with the meditations in the *Spiritual Exercises*.

Before Rembrandt painted *The Return of the Prodigal Son*, he painted *The Prodigal Son in the Tavern* in 1635 or 1636. He presented himself as the partying younger son and his wife Saskia as his companion. Durham is convinced this painting is based on the parable of the prodigal son in

6. Ibid., 24.
7. Ibid., 152.
8. Ibid., 60.
9. Ibid., 115–16.
10. Ibid., 118.

Light of Forgiveness

Luke 15 but doubts any specific message beyond the suggestion that none of us are immune to the temptations of prodigality.[11]

As we will see, the painting, *The Return of the Prodigal Son*, is Rembrandt's fullest confession of faith.[12] Rembrandt painted with high contrast by modeling in dark and white, a technique called chiaroscuro first used by Caravaggio. In this picture, the returning son kneels in front of his loving father. They are enveloped in light. Once again color imports spiritual light that emanates from the figures rather than from natural light. Look at the gold on the father's sleeves and his repentant son's robe. As Rembrandt ages, his palette became richer. "Dark red, brown and golden yellow were some of those he favored most."[13] The father's hands rest gently on his son's shoulders. This gesture of loving forgiveness is the artistic focal point and at the same time is the heart of the biblical story about the prodigal son in Luke 15:11–32. As you recall, a young man leaves home and squanders his share of his father's property. He hits bottom when he has to go to work on a pig farm. After returning home without any money, his father throws a party in celebration of the lost son returning home. His older brother is quite miffed.

Rembrandt painted a woman in the shadowy darkness behind the father on the left. A note of caution: Unless you have exceptional eyesight, you may not be able to see this woman in reproductions. I can sometimes see her in natural light. She is more easily seen in a black and white print in the 1963 version of *Art History* by H. W. Janson.

---

11. Ibid., 172.
12. Ibid., 177.
13. Watts, *Rembrandt*, 153.

Images of Light

Durham views her as possibly the mother.[14] He does not hint at deceit, as do some art historians.

Two men stand to the right of the father. Art historians have various opinions about the identity of these two men. I take my clues from the book *Reluctant Partners: Art and Religion in Dialogue,* edited by Ena Giurescu Heller of The Gallery at the American Bible Society in New York. Therefore I side with those who see the men as earlier versions of the father and elder son before the younger son took off in search of a partying life.

Intertextuality or comparing one text to another piece in the same work matters in biblical literature and in art. As passages in the Bible sometimes give hints of interpretation of other biblical passages, artists' paintings may be interpretative keys of other images in their work. Rembrandt based his painting on his drawing, *Isaac blessing Jacob.* Therefore because of artistic and biblical precedent, the woman in Rembrandt's painting of the prodigal son might be a symbol of deceit. As you recall, Jacob's mother Rebecca who was deceitful, showed Jacob how to steal his brother's birthright. The shape of the head of the prodigal son is strikingly similar to Jacob in the drawing.[15] This woman in the painting, who resembles Jacob's mother in the drawing, is not in the biblical story of the prodigal son. Rembrandt had some reason to include her. We are prompted to ask why? Could she be a symbol of deceit?

In Rembrandt's painting the prodigal son seems more pragmatic than truly repentant as Doug Adams observed. If so he could also be somewhat deceitful. To my eyes the son does seem shadowed and therefore possibly shady. Asking his father to treat him as a servant could mean just feed me as you do your servants, according to Doug Adams in

14. Durham, *The Biblical Rembrandt,* 176.
15. Heller, *Reluctant Partners,* 74.

Light of Forgiveness

his chapter, *Changing Perceptions of Jesus' Parables through Art History; Polyvalency in Paint*.[16] Adams goes on to say that Rembrandt emphasized the Reformation's insight that God's acceptance is based not on our merits but on grace and God's faith in us. Therefore a Protestant emphasis is often on the greatness of the Father's forgiveness. In Rembrandt's time the Catholic Council of Trent reacted to Protestant enthusiasm for the Father's forgiveness and emphasized repentance and encouraged artists to portray repentance so to encourage the sacrament of penance. Theological trends change. Nineteenth-century American Protestant preachers ran with the repentance theme.[17] Today being welcoming and accepting is a growing concern that dovetails with the theme of the father's and God's love.

There are multivalent or polyvalent interpretations of meanings in the painting and in identification of the characters. Different views can inform and enrich the others. One thought brought up in class is that the woman in the background might have been the mother, not at all deceitful, who like her husband wanted to welcome her youngest home. Or maybe the figure in the middle that could be a woman is not a servant[18] as a possibility that Durham suggests but the mother. My sense is that in class we did not even spot the woman in the upper left hand corner. If the woman in the middle or if the woman in the background, who is not deceitful, is the mother, then mother love is a positive image in the painting. Despite the confusion it is significant that there is a maternal presence. It was also suggested in class that maybe there were three sons (if the person in the middle is a male) and the two men were the eldest and middle sons.

16. Ibid., 76.
17. Ibid.
18. Durham, *The Biblical Rembrandt*, 176–77.

Images of Light

While acknowledging different emphases, I believe that the theme of the father's forgiveness is the most essential point. The emphasis on the father's love is clearly evident in my teenage thoughts. In the early sixties, the Rev. Edmund W. Nutting invited young people to write a short piece about the elder brother's attitude. In my essay that was published in the LOG, which is the newsletter of the First Congregational Church in Rockport, I wrote: "In the story of the Prodigal Son, the elder brother does not understand the real reason for his father's rejoicing. Perhaps he is thinking in terms of "'an eye for an eye' and 'a tooth for a tooth'" and thinks the merrymaking is a strange way to make amends for his brother's mistake. The Bible says (today I would say "it is written") that the oldest brother was angry. He also seemed jealous of his brother. His anger must have hindered his ability to understand the situation. The eldest son associated his father's love with a reward for something that was well done. He did not understand that the love was constant. The older brother did not realize that the merrymaking was the father's way of accepting a repentant son. If the story had continued, perhaps the younger brother would have helped his older brother understand the greatness of his father's love and forgiveness."

Here I am at age sixty-eight finding support as well as extended theological implications through painterly exegesis and Durham's insights for an essay that I wrote as a teenager. Durham's deep thought about *The Return of the Prodigal So*n gives me a fuller understanding of my own ponderings. In his conclusions about Rembrandt's painting, he wrote from the perspective of faith. "What Rembrandt gives us in *The Return of the Prodigal Son*, painted toward the end of his life, is the human face of God: the only face,

Light of Forgiveness

finally that any of us can really look upon and see."[19] The father's face is the essence of compassion.

A few years after writing my teenage essay, I found a challenging interpretation in a lithograph, *The Return,* by Philip Evergood. In 1966 the Division of Christian Education and the Division of Publication of the United Church Board for Homeland Ministries published a portfolio of lithographs titled *Christian Concepts in Art* with United Church Press. In 1967 I wrote a paper on these lithographs for a course in religious education taught by Dr. Wesner Fallaw at Andover Newton Theological School. One lithograph in the collection is titled *The Return* by Philip Evergood. Evergood (1907–1973) was an American painter, etcher, lithographer, sculptor and illustrator. He is known for his bold lines and for social realism. He was a figurative painter in an art world that places greater value on abstraction. However, during the 1950's Evergood departed from his established social realism and concentrated on both mythological and biblical symbolism. His father was Jewish but did not have a problem with Evergood's mother who was proud of her English heritage and wanted an English education for her son. She sent him to schools in England where he went to Episcopal services and read the Bible. In an oral history interview Evergood was asked about his biblical subject matter. Evergood said that it was a starting point for imagination. When asked by interviewer Forrest Selvig why not Shakespeare, Evergood replied, "Well, somehow Shakespeare would have made it too illustrative. I don't know why. I can't tell you why. Chaucer maybe might have been nearer to it for me. But I was frightened of the illustrative. I didn't want that. And I felt that the Bible when you take a subject like, oh, Shadrack, Meshach and Abednego

---

19. Ibid., 180.

in the fiery furnace you could take more liberties with that. Maybe it was that. I don't know."[20]

I said that in Philip Evergood's *The Return*, which is an abstract expressionist image of the faces of the father and prodigal son, there seems to be a note of judgment created by the father's eyes as well as acceptance. Looking again at this image in 2011, my sense was that the father is not blind to the faults of his son and while saddened by them still loves him deeply. He seems sad but not judgmental. The father's love is not blind, nor is God's. Reexamining art added more nuanced thought. Art like the written word can import meanings that evolve throughout life. From time to time reviewing the biblical story of the prodigal son as well as art and literature that explore the story can reveal new insights. Fresh sightings, like lighthouses, help all who must navigate through choppy waters.

Following the more dominant Protestant perspective, the Father's love is a symbol of God's love, which is so great that it is beyond total human understanding. Yet people do have a large measure of understanding based on experience as well as reading biblical stories. The father's forgiveness of his prodigal son, which symbolizes God's forgiveness, is the deepest compassion a human can experience. Two stories from two very different people who were moved by *The Return of the Prodigal Son* show responses of deepest gratitude and yearning for embrace and rest in acceptance.

The first story comes from Harry T. Cook in his book, *Resonance: Biblical Texts Speaking to 21st Century Inquirers*. When his daughter was ten, she often asked Harry to read her the parable of the Prodigal Son at bedtime. He never asked her why she liked the story, but one year she sent him a Father's Day card that suggests the appeal of the story. The

20. Oral history interview with Philip Evergood, 1968 Dec. 3, Archives of American Art, Smithsonian Institution.

Light of Forgiveness

message read: "For listening anytime, for believing every time, for loving me all the time...."[21]

The sins of the younger son were big and dramatic. Many of us have smaller and totally boring sins so the gift of forgiveness is not strongly felt. The perception of God as loving us all the time or gratitude for people who lovingly believe in us can be the embodiment of the love in the parable of the Prodigal Son. Acceptance from God or from other people in spite of our flaws is close to an experience of forgiveness. As theologian Paul Tillich wrote: "Simply accept the fact that you are accepted."[22] Accepting yourself may be easier said than done but keeping the thought is a start.

A woman who was the best reader of visual clues in my class noticed that the youngest son is wearing only one shoe. That other shoe is on the ground beside him. We all said in unison: "holy ground" and then "at least half holy ground." One barefooted son might be a reminder that the father is a holy man and a symbol of God but not God and that forgiveness is an earthly task. Asking people for forgiveness or finding a way to forgive ourselves is part of the process of reconciliation.

The second story comes from an article in "Boston College Magazine" about Henri Nouwen. Yes, he represents Catholicism yet his thought has an ecumenical flavor and a hint of a United Church of Christ open and affirming stance. He had just returned from a grueling six-week lecturing tour through the United States. He was exhausted. He happened to look at a large poster of Rembrandt's *The Return of the Prodigal Son*. He wrote:

---

21. Cook, *Resonance*, 14.
22. Tillich, *The Shaking of the Foundations*, 162.

Images of Light

> "My heart leapt when I saw it. After my long self-exposing journey, the tender embrace of father and son expressed everything I desired at that moment. I was, indeed, the son exhausted from long travels; I wanted to be embraced; I was looking for a home where I could feel safe. The son-come-home was all I was and all that I wanted to be. For so long I had been going from place to place: confronting, beseeching, admonishing, and consoling. Now I desired only to rest safely in a place where I could feel a sense of belonging, a place where I could feel at home."[23]

The first time when Nouwen was deeply moved by Rembrandt's *The Return of the Prodigal Son,* he identified with the younger son. Although Nouwen had been the model of dutiful and obedient, he yearned for the Father's embracing love and home in God's light. He wrote, "The father's embrace, full of light, is God's house."[24] Later a friend, Bart Gavigan,[25] pointed out to him that he was more like the self-righteous elder brother. Nouwen explored his inner elder brother stance and came to understand that the Father loved both sons. Then Nouwen discerned his need to grow up and become like the compassionate Father who did not compare one child to the other but loved both unconditionally. Nouwen pointed out that the compassionate father is also like a mother. The feminine dimension of God observed Nouwen is symbolized in the Father's caring right hand that to Nouwen is a tender, elegant mother's hand and

23. Waldron, *Still Life*, 48–49.
24. Nouwen, *The Return of the Prodigal Son*, 74.
25. Ibid., 20.

Light of Forgiveness

evokes words from the prophet Isaiah,[26] "Can a woman forget her nursing child, or show no compassion for the child of her womb? Even these may forget, yet I will not forget you. See, I have inscribed you on the palms of my hands . . ." (Isa 49:15–16). A man in my class noticed that the father's left hand is a huge working man's hand and indeed the right hand is that of a woman. I add that Isaiah's words were addressed to people in exile. Who among us has not felt exiled at some point in life? Mother loss is one kind of exile as are countless other kinds of loss. Rejection is a form of exile. Belonging to faith communities may be a balm.

For Nouwen, belonging to the household of God empowers us to be in the world.[27] To slightly paraphrase, people who can rejoice like God in the many small returns that people make are not cynical free from sorrow but have "pierced the meaning of true joy."[28] My take is that if you are able to believe that people can change, you can more fully trust that evolution is intent on betterment.

One paragraph forged by Nouwen is so important that I quote it in full. "People who have come to know the joy of God do not deny the darkness, but they chose not to live in it. They claim that the light that shines in the darkness can be trusted more than the darkness itself and that a little bit of light can dispel a lot of darkness. They point each other to flashes of light here and there, and remind each other that they reveal the hidden but real presence of God. They discover that there are people who heal each other's wounds, forgive each other's offenses, share their possessions, foster the spirit of community, celebrate the gifts they

---

26. Ibid., 99.
27. Ibid., 116.
28. Ibid., 117.

have received, and live in constant anticipation of the full manifestation of God's glory."[29]

In summary, a sense of home, acceptance, and belonging were the import of Rembrandt's painting for Nouwen. Feeling at home in the world can mean assurance of God's loving forgiveness or conviction that ultimately the universe is friendly enough that we can forgive ourselves. The lights of forgiveness, acceptance, and belonging can change hearts and the world.

Reflection

Thoughtful people in my class said that the younger son was a young man who messed up. He did not molest children. We all agreed that belief in God's unconditional love does not mean a free pass. For years I have thought that Matthew's reporting of Jesus's instruction to Peter to forgive seventy-seven times (18:22) means that forgiveness is a process. If forgiveness for people, who are made in God's image is a process, it may be a process for God also. Unconditional love and acceptance may not mean instantaneous forgiveness.

Sometimes a thought in the bible counterbalances another contrasting idea although not always with equal weight. Readers will surely want to point out to me that the writer of the Letter to the Ephesians counsels his readers to never let the sun go down on their anger (4:2). That passage has been causing controversy since the first century! In my view Jesus trumps the writer of Ephesians who was writing in Paul's name. Perhaps such a quick resolution of conflict was the hope of a first-century church leader who wanted to

---

29. Ibid.

Light of Forgiveness

mend conflict immediately! Or as Rev. Jim quipped, "Probably he had been to a church council meeting!"

Questions

1. Do you think that forgiveness is a process?
2. Have you had an experience of forgiveness or acceptance that you wish to share?
3. Are there people who have been there for you and believed in you?
4. Can you identify places of safety and sanctuary?
5. Does your faith help you to feel at home in this world?
6. Do you identify with the younger brother, the elder brother or the father?
7. Do you feel that the younger brother was or could have been devious?
8. How do you respond to Nouwen's statement that the light is God's house?
9. Has anyone given you a glimmer of light?
10. Have you had to struggle with forgiving anyone?
11. Does the painting of the prodigal son express something important to you or an alternate experience, perspective, or reality?
12. Do hands in the painting take on symbolic meaning for you?
13. Does the painting offer you comfort, consolation, or compensation?

Images of Light

ONLINE RESOURCES

1. www.rembrandtonline.org Then go to The Complete Works
2. Try: List of paintings by Rembrandt—Wikipedia

Luke 10

4

Light of Caring

The Good Samaritan (After Delacroix)
Vincent van Gogh
1890
oil on canvas
28 3/4 by 23 5/8 in
Kroller-Muller Museum
Otterlo, The Netherlands

As you have seen, yellow-gold in my dream foreshadowed golden images in this book. Yellow-gold will burst forth into fullest glory in the final chapter on the light of the resurrection. For now, yellow gold is a symbol of the divine spark in human life or a taste of the eternal now or "glory divine." As I finished up this essay I thought best to look at a collage I made in 1994. Because I forgot the composition and colors, I was amazed to find the exact golden-yellow in my dream. The canvas in my collage is golden-yellow with colored rice paper pasted onto the canvas. You can imagine the yellow in the black and white illustration. The line in back of the Good Samaritan is golden-yellow. The same yellow is at the top right and suggests transcendent light. The yellow line flows through the Good Samaritan. In color you can see the yellow band through his body. God's love flows into him and creates a moment of divine caring in human life.

Good Samaritan, Sharon R. Chace

As you probably have heard in sermons, there are different New Testament words for love. Philo is friendship and related to our word Philadelphia, the city of brotherly and sisterly love. Eros means erotic love. Agape is God's

Light of Caring

love, which is expressed biblically in the love of neighbor. My simplified explanation of agape love is caring across the gaps of north and south, east and west, friend and enemy. The Good Samaritan actualizes agape love. Agape love is the eternal in the now. You may wonder if I made the collage to express ideas about divine love flowing into people. No. I first crafted the image and then discovered what I meant and put my thoughts into words. The syntax of images came before verbal understanding of my thoughts.

The Good Samaritan in van Gogh's painting and in biblical literature depicts the light of caring that brightens darkness. This painting can help us on our ascent to trust that goodness will prevail over darkness. As you recall from your reading of Luke's story about a Good Samaritan (10:25-37), a Levite and a priest saw a man who had been beaten, robbed, and abandoned by the side of a road. I can still remember the words from a dramatic reading created by Mrs. Greenwood, who was the wife of Minister Emeritus Rev. Dr. Walter Greenwood, for girls in the Pilgrim Fellowship of First Congregational in Rockport to read together (c.1960). Speaking of the robbers, we recited in unison: "And they beat him and departed, leaving him half dead." As you recall, a Levite and a priest passed by but a Samaritan who was among those despised by the Jews stopped to help the man left by the side of the road. At the time I felt that the reading was overly dramatic but also sensed that the reading would help us remember a significant New Testament story.

Matthew (22 34-40), Mark (12:28-34), and Luke (10:25-37) recount Jesus' citation of Deut 6:4-5 that stresses loving God with heart, understanding (or mind) and strength and neighbor as one's self. Mark, who is strongly tied to his Jewish ancestors, prefaces his statement with the words, "Hear, O Israel: the Lord our God, is one." Luke develops the definition of neighbor. Whether Luke's expansions reflect Jesus' exact words or is artistic Luke's literary creation, the message is crucial for humanity.

Van Gogh painted the story. However, his painting is not a mere illustration because it penetrates the surface and reveals service as having ultimate meaning. In 1964 there was an ecumenical arts week in Rockport centered mostly at St. Mary's Episcopal Church. Dr. Samuel H. Miller, at the time the Dean of Harvard Divinity School, spoke. According to an article in the *Gloucester Daily Times*, issue of August 19, 1964, written by an unnamed Rockport reporter, Dr. Miller said that great artists try to get behind the surface appearances to the reality beneath. I was there and believe he gave credit to Paul Tillich, which would have been fair. (For a short treatment on Tillich on art see the book, *Art, Creativity, and the Sacred*, edited by Diane Apostolos-Cappadona.) Miller, like Tillich, saw religious art not so much as subject matter but as revelation of ultimate concerns. Van Gogh painted religious subject matter that reveals significant realities.

Sometimes a person's funeral or memorial service captures a person's life. So it was with van Gogh's service. Kathleen Powers Erickson tells us that Emile Bernard described the funeral of his dear friend van Gogh to Albert Aurier, who was the first to acknowledge van Gogh's genius, noting the importance of light, the color yellow and the symbol of the sunflower in van Gogh's life and work.[1] Bernard wrote: "On the coffin a simple white linen, masses of flowers, the sunflowers which he loved so much, yellow dahlias, yellow flowers everywhere. It was his favorite color, as you will remember, a symbol of the light he dreamt in hearts as well as

---

1. Erickson, *At Eternity's Gate*, 182

Light of Caring

in paintings."[2] Yellow often implied a divine presence.[3] You may have already sensed the significance of gold through your own observation of van Gogh's popular sunflowers. The immense amount of primary resources that Erickson used in her book will fill out the meanings and impact of yellow-gold in van Gogh's work.

Colors in Van Gogh's *The Good Samaritan* contribute to meanings. One would expect the almost dead man to be pale yet so are the Levite and the priest. The implication might be that religious hypocrisy is a form of death. Yet there are signs of life. Look at the jewel-tone, stained glass window colors in the picture. You can imagine light shining through the colors brightening the scene of both neglect and caring. The Samaritan wears a ruby-red hat and is robed in sapphire blue and orange-citrine. Robed in the same blue as the Samaritan, the beaten man, as well as the Samaritan, is enfolded in God's presence suggested by heavenly blue.

There is yellow-gold in the trees and on the path to and from the Temple in Jerusalem. Although the Levite and the priest in van Gogh's painting had been or were on the upward climb to Jerusalem, they were not on the high road to spiritual re-birth. The biblical account says that the priest was going down the road, which might imply that he was going home. Daniel J. Harrington wrote: "The story of Luke 10:30–35 may assume that the priest and the Levite were returning from Jerusalem after having taken their turns in the rites at the Temple. There is some remote possibility that their refusal to minister to the wounded man was due to their fear of ritual impurity brought about by contact with a corpse. On the other hand, the Samaritan came from the

2. Ibid., 182. Quoted in Jan Hulsker, *Vincent and Theo van Gogh*, 447.

3. Ibid., 76.

Images of Light

area of Palestine situated between Galilee and Judea. Suspected of being a 'non-Jew' by the Judeans, the Samaritan plays the role of the foreigner over against the priest and the Levite."[4] In any case the priest and the Levite were not caring, inclusive, nor open and affirming. To my mind, in order to avoid any anti-Jewish sentiment it is important to remember that the priest and the Levite could be any of us.

The path reminds me that Erickson stresses the impact of John Bunyan's *The Pilgrim's Progress* on van Gogh's work, for example in *Crows over the Wheatfield*.[5] The roads through the wheat symbolize the journey. The wheat symbolizes rebirth in the cycle of life and is a subtle reference to the divine presence in the Eucharist, writes Erickson. Erickson also said that like Christian in Bunyan's allegory, van Gogh viewed temporal existence as an arduous journey that would ultimately end in spiritual rebirth.[6] In this painting van Gogh expressed sorrow as well as a sense of release as his life journey came to an end. Yet he persisted in his belief in rest and peace beyond the grave.[7]

Van Gogh was a missionary minister for a short time until he was let go because clerical leaders were not pleased with his severe asceticism, which was a life style of extreme poverty. Van Gogh's choice of the subject matter for the Good Samaritan was both his rejection of the hypocrisy of Christian clergy and continued commitment to serving the poor that started in his days of ministry.[8] Erickson explains that the *Good Samaritan* displays van Gogh's personal concern for deliverance from sickness. As the Good Samaritan was rescued and restored to health van Gogh hoped for the

4. Harrington, *Interpreting the New Testament*, 7.
5. Erickson, *At Eternity's Gate*, 160–62.
6. Ibid., 160–61.
7. Ibid., 148.
8. Ibid., 159.

Light of Caring

same deliverance.[9] Converging with van Gogh's hopes for deliverance, some church fathers interpreted the Good Samaritan as Jesus and viewed the care of the wounded man as symbolic of the care that God (and Jesus) shows to all kinds of people.[10] Since it seems clear that Luke who crafted the story and Jesus himself instruct us to be good Samaritans, the interpretation of some of the church fathers may strike us as counter-intuitive. Interpretations need not be seen as chemically pure. Perhaps Jesus did see himself aligned with the caring of the Good Samaritan. When people care for one another, as did the Good Samaritan, the divine spark shines brightly. Being like Jesus for others is participation in light.

My observation that converges with van Gogh's experience is that if the Levite and the priest stopped to help, they would have participated in the light of caring that was outside of their institutional religion. Van Gogh did not always have faith in the institutional church. He viewed the whitewashed wall as symbol of hypocrisy.[11] The church in *Starry Night* is not lit.[12] For those of us who love our whitewashed, Puritan meeting house walls, I suggest that the positive message is that the clear windows let in the sunlight and sometimes views of other steeples. Also we are free to find our own sustaining images that are not paintings or stained glass pictures that have been around for three hundred years. People in charge of flowers work wonders in the selection of plants to go on the windowsills of clear glass windows, especially at Easter. White Easter lilies are pristine. Tulips and daffodils are especially lovely when backlit by morning light.

9. Ibid., 159–60.
10. Harrington, *Why Do We Hope?*, 84.
11. Erickson, *At Eternity's Gate*, 180.
12. Ibid., 170–71.

Images of Light

To my eye the saturated colors in the Good Samaritan are full-bodied and Christian faith expressed in the painting is also full-bodied. Erickson tells us that in the *Good Samaritan* van Gogh wove the rich, vibrant coloring of Delacroix's romantic history painting with splashes of crimson, sapphire, and gold, into the more subdued tones of brown, grays, and red-ocher that recall the palette for his Dutch past.[13] Thus while van Gogh's composition is that of Delacroix, he infuses the composition with his own pathos and synthesis of his experiences of colors that include the favored hues from his Dutch past and the lighter, more gentle colors of the impressionists. In my class an observant woman noticed the streaks of white from sky to ground in back of the horse's head. Erickson speaks about the importance of white light as opposed to whitewashed walls for van Gogh. After he left the church and began to see a difference between "true" and "false" religion, he saw some people as a black ray of light and others as a white ray. His father and uncle were of the black ray type and Millet above all others had white light. Van Gogh had faith in ultimate light winning, "I see God, who is the White Ray of Light, who has the Last Word."[14]

Blue is a significant color in van Gogh's paintings. Considering blue in *Starry Night* can help us more fully appreciate blue in the *Good Samaritan*. He used the intense blue of the sky as a symbol of the divine and infinite presence, especially in *Starry Night*.[15] Because blue in the background ties the Samaritan and the victim to the blue hills rising up to the sky, the whole painting is to my eyes filled with God. *Starry Night*, says Erickson, represents the mystic's

13. Ibid., 160.
14. Ibid., 78–80.
15. Ibid., 82.

Light of Caring

desire for union with the infinite God.[16] In this painting van Gogh created an image of divine love and immensity of the cosmos. The stars in their courses that intimated immortality gave him hope and comfort.[17] I am reminded by Paul's words that he quoted from poets before him in Acts 17:28: "For 'In him we live and move and have our being'; as even some of your own poets have said, 'For we too are his offspring.'" Paul, van Gogh, and ancient poets seem to share mystical intimations of the divine. In case anyone is wondering, I do also. Although I no longer believe that God is all-powerful, in my experience the mystery in which we live and move and have our being enfolds a guiding and loving force that I call God. While acknowledging an inner editor in my subconscious mind who is personal because my subconscious must care about me, I cannot limit guidance to just DNA directing the unfolding of my life. Because there have been so many moments of help coming with a sense of divine presence that seem to me to be more than coincidences, I cannot claim that God is only in my mind, heart, and imagination. Adapting Harry T. Cook's words in his online essay of July 13, 2012, I think that my beliefs are metaphoric approximations of what may be true. With that provision I can sing gospel hymns with abandon.

In her book, *At Eternity's Gate: The Spiritual Vision of Vincent van Gogh*, Kathleen Powers Erickson gives important information to art lovers and people of faith by telling us that van Gogh read Thomas a Kempis's *The Imitation of Christ* and presents the ethics of Kempis in *The Good Samaritan*.[18] Erickson goes on to say that van Gogh read in Kempis's *The Imitation of Christ* that in summary it is good to remember that you came to religion to serve and not to

16. Ibid., 165.
17. Ibid., 166.
18. Ibid., 159.

be served. To my mind spiritual writers and artists as well as biblical exegetes offer helpful insights about biblical stories.

Erickson's discussion of the Samaritan's horse is worthy of reading and re-reading. She said that it may have been van Gogh's intention that the horse would become an emblem of Kempis's ideal of the long suffering Christian servant.[19] She goes on to say that van Gogh wrote to his sister, Wil, wondering if she had noticed that the old cab horses in Paris had large beautiful eyes like some brokenhearted Christians. I have a very old Phaidon Press book, *Van Gogh*, which belonged to my mother. The plate of *The Good Samaritan* is in black and white. The black and white plate brings out the horse's eyes, which struck me as being like the compassionate eyes of Christ. The horse is also a seer who looks deeply into the nature of life as did Vincent van Gogh.

In contrast to the passive and patient suffering of the horse, it seems to me that the Good Samaritan is an action hero. Patient endurance shown by the horse, social action exemplified by the Good Samaritan, caring people, and trust in a caring God can all be part of life in Christ. People are lifted beyond their preoccupations by the light of caring.

On a personal note, when the Chace family needed help, we learned that there are people in the world who are good Samaritans. At the time, Ernie was the pastor of First Congregational Church (UCC) in Verona, New Jersey. On Easter Sunday afternoon in 1978 on the way to visit family in Rockport, we were literally in the ditch when our 1972 Dodge Dart broke down at the exit off the George Washington Bridge in New York City. Good people from the Bronx who lived behind the gas station gave us a radiator hose. The German shepherd, guard dog at the Gulf station, took to us and even let me pet him! He looked at us with his big

19. Ibid., 160.

Light of Caring

brown eyes. The horse that mattered to Van Gogh had tired eyes from sadness or exhausting service. So did the dog. What he saw with his tired, pensive eyes I do not know. The gas station attendant had the mind of the Good Samaritan and of Christ. May we look with compassion and have the mindfulness to extend a hand of caring. The light of caring brightens the ascent to the mountaintop of triumph.

Questions

1. Do you identify either with the Good Samaritan or with the man at the side of the road?
2. Has anyone been a Good Samaritan to you?
3. Have you been a Good Samaritan to others?
4. Not everyone has the physical strength like the Good Samaritan to lift an injured person onto a horse or onto an ambulance stretcher. How do you imagine your ways of helping?
5. Does interpreting the Good Samaritan as Jesus or God help you to feel that you do not have to do everything by yourself?
6. Does interpreting the Good Samaritan as God or as Jesus help you to feel God's presence or the support of other people when you are in need of healing or deliverance from trouble?
7. Does the painting express something you have seen or experienced?
8. Does the painting offer consolation or comfort or compensation for something lacking in your experience?

Matthew 8–9; Mark 1–2;
Luke 8; Revelation 22

5

Light of Healing

The Tree of Life
Henri Matisse
1949
As cut-out for the
Apse in the Chapel of the Rosary
202 3/4 by 99 1/8 in
The Vatican Museums,
Collection of Modern Religious Art

The Tree of Life
Henri Matisse
1949
As cut-out for the
Nave in the Chapel of the Rosary
202 3/4 by 202 3/4 in
The Vatican Museums,
Collection of Modern Religious Art

Images of Light

> ". . . and the leaves of the tree
> are for the healing of the nations."
>
> —Revelation 22:2

HEALING WAS PART OF Jesus' ministry. Today there are kinds of healing that Jesus could not imagine. Yet healing in many forms is part of the on-going spirit of Christ, the mythic hero, who was true to himself and willing to die for his beliefs. In so doing he opened up his ethics to a wider world if you are a humanist and ethical monotheism if you are a theist. Because Jesus shows us the best way to live, his example is healing and saving. Finding one's task that is informed and infused with the ethics of Jesus is one kind of healing. Maturing into being loving and forgiving is also healing and saving. Therefore ethics and attitudes: sharing and caring are healing for the helpers and for people who are served.

While not in denial of nature's destructive side, healing also comes through natural beauty. By evoking feelings of wholeness, or being one with God or with the universe, light shining through leaves on trees is healing. Healing of body and spirit is saving. In nature and in art, trees connect earth and heaven. Looking up at the light, people may intuit transcendence.

Beauty can be revelatory. Immersion in light can be sacramental. Blessing comes in glimpses of the sacred.

I suspect that Sister Jacques-Marie, the nun who nursed the ailing Matisse, knew that Matisse's colors and shapes in his cut-out designs could mediate grace to receiving souls. She asked him to design a window for the chapel that the nuns were building in Vence, France. Matisse's art

Light of Healing

is more than decorative. He was aligned with a tradition of poetic and pastoral art that stresses restoration of people with tired spirits and also with universal harmony.[1] Listen to Matisse in his own words. "What I dream of is an art of balance, of purity and serenity devoid of troubling or depressing subject-matter, an art which might be for every mental worker, be he businessman or writer, like an appeasing influence, like a mental soother, something like a good armchair in which to rest from physical fatigue."[2] A woman in my class said that the aquatic shapes in Matisse's collages reminded her of the fish and birds that comforted children in cancer wards where she worked as an occupational therapist. Art can comfort and console. When not everything in life is beautiful, pastoral images in art can compensate.

Not all people share the same sensibilities. I must note a perspective that is vastly different from mine. Even though people in my class had similar perceptions of comforting color, I cannot make our experience into a universal claim. For me color is intrinsically important. Embracing color as a gift is my style of spirituality, which can be defined as response to grace or other forms of transcendent good will. If I found myself in hospice care, the most important art book for me to have with me would be *The Cut-outs of Henri Matisse* by John Elderfield because I could look at the images and soak in the colors. Even without knowing about Matisse's illness that brought out his work, his cut-outs would still speak to me. That is not to say that his biography is not important yet for me it is secondary. For other people it remains primary. Timothy Hyman, reviewing Richard Cork's book *The Healing Presence of Art: A History of Western Art in Hospitals*, speaks of Van Gogh, Edward Munch, and Matisse as (former) hospital patients who painted for self-expression, [in contrast to painters who had been

---

1. Elderfield, *The Cut-outs of Henri Matisse*, 38.
2. Goldwater and Treves, *Artists on Art*, 413.

commissioned to paint pictures to console soldiers, seamen, and sick people] the reviewer said that if their works still perform any healing function, "it will be because they appear as the tragic protagonists—as the wounded shamans of our own society."[3]

I struggle with the thought because Matisse was commissioned to design the Chapel of the Rosary, which must have deeply mattered to ailing communicants. Nevertheless the role of tragic protagonist and their biographies suggests to me that life-stories can be healing.

Therefore it seems to me that some people need biographies with exemplary protagonists and others are sustained by color. These needs are not mutually exclusive.

Too sick to paint, Matisse drew with scissors cutting out shapes from brightly colored paper that were translated into stained glass. *The Tree of Life* windows in both the nave and the apse are done in joyous colors; happy spring green, golden and lemon-yellow, cobalt, and sapphire blue. The yellow amoeboid leaves in the apse stand out, inviting you into sacred space and insisting on blessedness. Imagine gentle breezes softly blowing through the leaves refreshing you. It is as if Matisse is saying, "lay your burdens down and enter into the joy of healing light. Know that joy is deeper than both sorrow and happiness."

Matisse wanted his cut-outs done with brightly colored paper that are the designs for the stained glass windows in the Chapel of the Rosary to go to a museum after his death. In 1980 his son Pierre gave them to the Vatican. Kept in storage for thirty years they are now in a special room at the Vatican that has special lighting to bring out the best blue and yellow. I am overjoyed to tell my readers that you can see the cut-outs online. The easiest way is to

3. Hymen, "Painters' Rites," review of *The Healing Presence in Art*, 11.

Light of Healing

enter your online search with the words: Vatican museum opens unique Matisse display.[4]

Matisse had a kindred spirit who painted in a very different time and place. In 1811 an itinerant artist, John Avery, who was born in 1790, painted a beautiful wrap-around mural of trees in the original, Free-Will Baptist meeting house of Middleton, New Hampshire. Dark green leaves with yellow-green leaves in back of the darker ones suggest sponge painting or a similar process with a dry brush or rags. The yellow green in back of the darker green against the yellow-beige walls implies morning light. Mountains of New Hampshire are hinted at in curly, rounded lines with a bit of golden shading that appears to be faded. Mustard yellow is his signature color for backgrounds and is even more pronounced in the Captain Enoch Remick house in nearby Tamworth. Avery's rounded mountains and combination of yellow and green converge with Matisse's shapes and colors.

Matisse's amoeboid yellow leaves stand out against blue oval-like leaves and a bright green background. Matisse's and Avery's leaves and light have symbolic import suggesting healing and life. There are artificial yet life-like trees with dark green leaves similar to Avery's painted leaves on trees behind the altar in the Unitarian Universalist Society in Rockport, Massachusetts. Leaves in the sacred spaces of the Roman Catholic chapel, and now the Vatican, a Free Will Baptist meeting house and a Unitarian Universalist society suggest a shared visual language that connotes healing in nature. Leaves and light may be close to universal symbols with bridge-building potential to heal humanity wounded by divisions.

---

4. Video footage of Matisse's cutouts can be viewed online at http://www.romereports.com.

Images of Light

Detail of John Avery Mural,
photograph by Ernest S. Chace

Matisse believed that the chapel was his masterpiece. He explained that "All art worthy of the name is religious."[5] Working on the designs for the chapel did not cure his cancer, but life completed by using his talents to the glory of God was saving and healing. Healing from living his life

5. O'Roark, "A Beautiful Place," 45.

Light of Healing

well was spiritually saving. As Harry T. Cook reminds us, the New Testament Greek word for salvation connotes healing.[6] Matisse accepted his physical limitation and went on to do his greatest work. He shared his colors and his cut-outs. I believe that for us artists, sacrifice or dedication or offering means using up all our crayons.

Healing can be more than a cure. Sometimes peace with things as they are is healing. Years ago before I understood that being an incubator baby and getting too much oxygen would mean very slow physical development, my sister Rosemary wisely said to me that my life-long lack of stamina and coordination is just the way things are and we do not have to know all the reasons. Despite lack of explanations, there was partial healing in Rosemary's acceptance of me and in my budding acceptance of myself. In time further healing and purpose unfolded when I decided it was best to use my limited strength for graduate work rather than attempting to drive to the IGA in an effort to be "as normal as possible." Purpose became more defined during my graduate days at Weston Jesuit School of Theology. I learned that the best way for me to contribute to religious education is through writing.

I deduced that cure and healing are not the same on my own. By chance, serendipity, or perhaps divine providence, shortly after writing a few drafts of this essay, I read a review of *Partners in Care: Ministry and Medicine Together*, by Frederick Reklau, who makes 14 thesis statements and then backs them up not so much as proof but as evidence that opens up discussions about his ideas and the complementary roles of doctors and ministers.[7] Three of these main ideas that seem to me to apply to Matisse are: 1. Cure may occur without healing; healing may occur with-

---

6. Cook, *Long Live Salvation By Works*, 15–16.
7. Reklau, *Partners in Care: Medicine and Ministry Together*, 43.

out cure. (Matisse's last work must have been healing.) To my mind Reklau's definition of healing is more suggestive than clearly defined. (Serenity is my take on his definition.) 2. Cure fosters function; healing fosters purpose. (Matisse certainly found deepened purpose in his work towards the end of his life when he had intestinal cancer and did not seem to have a future.) 3. Cure encounters mystery as a challenge for understanding; healing encounters mystery as a channel for meaning. (Matisse's cut-outs evoke a sense of mystery through color and light.) I recommend this book to clergy, doctors, nurses, health care workers, and anyone who is interested in the work of doctors and clergy.

While having never viewed Matisse's original trees of life, even in reproductions the colors, shapes, and imagined light shining through are so beautiful that anything that is, or could be, wrong in my life vanishes at least for the moments of contemplation. There is artistic communion, even a Eucharistic moment. Deep speaks to deep. Matisse's vision of the biblical tree of life is an invitation to earthly rest in God. In letting go of worries, peace is inner light.

Questions for Discussion

1. Have you had moving experiences of light or color?
2. Matisse said that his cut-out designs were the most simple and direct way to express himself. What is your most simple and direct way of expressing yourself?
3. What do you think it means to say that all art that is worthy of the name is religious?
4. Have you experienced healing?
5. Do you feel that there is a difference between cure and healing?

6. Do you feel comfort or consolation when looking at Matisse's cut-outs?

An Art Project

Think about colors that have sustained you and cut out colored shapes from construction paper, other papers, and old magazines. The shapes can be pasted onto white or black or any solid color poster-board in two different ways. Firstly, the shapes could be combined into one design. Secondly, the poster-board could be broken up into a grid pattern and each participant could fill in one section. The grid could be in squares or diamond shapes. The overall design might imply more emphasis on community and the individual squares or diamond shapes could suggest focus on the individual. However, I really think the choice of design is more a matter of temperament than theological emphasis. Engineers and quilt makers will likely prefer grids. Artists, especially those who majored in art in the 1960s when the emphasis was on abstract expressionism will probably favor a single design.

Speaking Truth to Power

Matthew 26–27; Mark 14–15;
Luke 23; John 18

6

Light of Truth

Christ Before the High Priest
Gerrit van Honthorst
c. 1617
oil on canvas
107 by 72 ins
National Gallery, London

GERRIT VAN HONTHORST'S MASTERPIECE, *Christ Before the High Priest*, is a cultural cliché and a monumental metaphor. As a cliché and as a painterly metaphor it connotes the light of truth. Honthorst was a Dutch follower of Caravaggio who taught Honthorst how to paint with modeling in dark and light. Honthorst made candlelight scenes very popular. Lighted candle scenes are meaningful even to this day. Just because with extensive use candle scenes have become a cliché does not mean that candle images do not convey truth. Remember all the Christmas cards you have received with pictures of a lighted candle! Perhaps as a child in Sunday school you took part in a children's

Images of Light

worship service. There may have been an altar in the worship space that was a table covered in a light blue cloth with an open Bible in front of a lighted candle. Lighted candles bring to mind the saying that is now part of our culture, "It is better to light one little candle than curse the dark." John's words come from strongest trust in the promises of Christmas and of Easter: "The light shines in the darkness, and the darkness did not overcome it" (1:5).

This painting is a monumental metaphor. It is monumental because it addresses an on-going issue of the human condition, which is the continual need to speak truth to power. As a visual metaphor, the painting is open to interpretation and stimulates imaginative rather than purely, rational, analytic thought.

In this painting the high priest who is Caiaphas in Matthew's gospel and I assume Caiaphas in this picture, and Jesus are facing each other. Jesus and Caiaphas look intelligent although Jesus is silently contemplative and Caiaphas appears to be aggressive with his upward finger of authority. Both have red cloth on their shoulders, which can be an artistic suggestion of power albeit of different kinds. The red patches are an artistic device that joins two sections of the painting together. The joining of the two sections tightens the connection between Jesus and Caiaphas. Jesus and Caiaphas are linked forever in this picture and in the New Testament. The light source is the lighted candle in front of an open book. The book is not the type of book that was used in the time of Jesus. It could be the Bible that Dutch Calvinists diligently studied. I wish I could say it seems to be open to suffering servant images in Isaiah but it is more likely opened to Job. I came to this conclusion by opening my Bible to about the same place as the book in the painting. In either case, the open book may suggest Jesus as loyal to God and patient in suffering as was Job. Faithfulness to

Light of Truth

God and patience in suffering can be appropriate stances when addressing power. More pro-active movements may at times be the best way to speak truth to power. More light shines on Jesus than on Caiaphas. Therein is encouragement to speak and to act. The light of speaking truth to power can enlighten the world and flow into societal transfiguration.

Questions

1. How do you voice your concerns to those in power in religious or political power?
2. During your lifetime, when, where, why, and how have you questioned or confronted authority in church or society?
3. Have there been stepping stones of social concern on your spiritual journey?

*Transfiguration
and Resurrection*

Matthew 17; Mark 9; Luke 9

7

Light of the Transfiguration

Sailing Boats
Lyonel Feininger
1929
oil on canvas
17 by 28 in
Detroit Institute of Arts

The Glorious Victory of the Sloop "Maria"
Lyonel Feininger
1926
oil on canvas
21 1/2 by 33 1/2 in
City Art Museum of St. Louis

IN MARK'S ACCOUNT OF the transfiguration (9:2–13), Jesus along with Peter, James, and John climbs a high mountain. Jesus was transformed. Mark tells us that Jesus' clothes became "dazzling white, such as no one on earth could bleach them" (9:3). Mark did not use unnecessary words. His gospel is concise and fast-paced. He was not one to be slowed down by adding unnecessary information. Therefore this color detail has to be important. As an artist I say that transformation white was titanium white or the brightest white copy paper in the office supply store. Moses and Elijah were also there as good company for Jesus and also as forefathers who were in their historical time truth-speakers and freedom seekers. The frightened yet awe-struck disciples proposed a shrine to prolong the experience. Institutional religion was not what was on Jesus' mind. Nor did Jesus' disciples understand that he was about to suffer and to die.

In the mystical moment when Jesus was bathed in radiant white light, a voice from a cloud re-identifies Jesus as God's Son. Jesus was identified as God's Son at baptism but Peter, James, and John were not there to hear that announcement. Moses and Elijah disappeared. Truth and freedom dissolved into light. The historical Jesus was transformed into Christ the mythic hero whose teachings continue to lighten and lift. Brightest white can be a symbol of transfiguration of the world. Transfiguration can mean figuring out how systems work and when necessary rearranging them. There is triumph in transfiguration.

This is a difficult story. The only features I feel certain of are that the white symbolizes the ultimate glorification of Jesus and that Mark who was the most emotional evangelist glimpsed the importance of white. My sense is that the whiteness in Mark also unintentionally foreshadows light in Revelation. Sometimes biblical writers say more than they know. The righteous will be clothed in white robes (Rev 3:5). In the heavenly city the glory of the Lord is light (Rev 21:23). You will recall Henri Nouwen's belief that light is God's house. Light as foreshadowing suggests a future or eschatological dimension of the light of Christ to transform the cosmos into a holy dwelling.

Light of the Transfiguration

Lyonel Feininger began drawing around 1893 when he was a small boy and started to paint in oils in 1907. His patterned glowing colors are luminous and dream-like. In Feininger's paintings, ships and churches, skyscrapers and sea are bathed in pristine light. Nature becomes mystical. His painting, *Sailing Boats*, does not have explicit religious subject matter, yet it imports the ultimate victory of light over darkness. Perhaps his own art and personal integrity sustained him when the Nazis labeled his art degenerate. He had to leave Germany, which was home to the Bauhaus; where in 1919 he was the first appointed faculty member by Walter Gropius. Testifying to hope in goodness, bright white light is the focal point and is infused throughout the painting. Two triangular sails are done in soft, warm, golden tones that reflect sunlight. The undulating waves flow in overlapping triangular shapes. The triangle shapes behind the sailboats are luminous in sunset shades of pink and blue. The beauty of nature is transformed into the beauty of math. In turn geometry is transfigured with beauty of light and color. Essences speak of what is most important and enduring. Light as essence is in itself a form of victory.

Because Feininger's work has private meanings, it seems to me, he would expect that his viewers would interpret personally. In another painting, *The Glorious Victory of the Sloop "Maria"*, three figures in the foreground stand together looking into the light that permeates geometric shapes of sea and sails. The light in this picture also turns the geometric shapes into sacred geometry for people who see truth and beauty in mathematics. Although it is most unlikely that the artist intended the figures to be Jesus, Moses, and Elijah, they come to mind. At the same time these figures could be any of us who yearn for mountain top, mystical moments of unity with God or all humanity when

Images of Light

it is possible to trust in triumphant light, despite whatever is ahead in life.

Questions

1. Have you had mystical moments?
2. Is light an important symbol for you?

Matthew 28; Luke 24; John 20

8

Light of Resurrection

Resurrection
Matthias Grünewald
c.1510
oil on wood
106 by 56 in
Unterlinden Museum, Colmar, Germany

The Virgin and Child with St. George and St. Anthony Abbott
Antonio Pisanello
c. 1450s
tempera on wood
18 1/2 x 11 in
National Gallery, London

The Supper at Emmaus
Vincenzo Catena
1520/30
oil on canvas
51 by 94 3/4 in
Galleria degli Uffizi, Florence

Images of Light

> *Pietà* (after Delacroix)
> Vincent van Gogh
> 1889
> oil on canvas
> 28 3/4 by 23 3/4 in
> Van Gogh Museum, Amsterdam

> *The Raising of Lazarus* (after Rembrandt)
> Vincent van Gogh
> 1890
> oil on canvas
> 19 1/4 by 24 3/4 in
> Van Gogh Museum, Amsterdam

NOT EVERY RELIGIOUS JOURNEY ends in martyrdom but every person will die. Some people feel that rest after a life well lived is reward enough. I contemplate a minister's gravestone in the Springbrook cemetery of Mansfield, Massachusetts, which says simply REST. Other people yearn for more than peace at the end of the journey.

Whether you view the resurrection of Jesus as bodily or spiritual, or understand resurrection for yourself as continuous in another realm or mattering forever because of your work for the reign of fairness and forgiveness, I offer reflections. My observations about colors may sustain your hopes for the future or give meaning in the present. These colors are yellow and blue.

Yellow, a happy color, appears in pictures of resurrection or implied resurrection. Five pictures for consideration are: *Resurrection* by Matthias Grünewald, *The Virgin and Child with St. George and St. Anthony Abbott* by Antonio Pisanello, *The Supper at Emmaus* by Vincenzo Catena, *Pietà*

Light of Resurrection

(after Delacroix) by Vincent van Gogh, and *The Raising of Lazarus* (after Rembrandt) by Vincent van Gogh.

Matthias Grünewald was a German Renaissance painter who continued the expressive style of late medieval European art. He is most famous for the Isenheim Altarpiece. The altarpiece illustrates the same intensity of religious feelings that motivated reformers like Martin Luther.[1]

Grünewald, the German artist, was commissioned by Frenchmen, the monks of the Antonite monastery to be exact.[2] This connection strikes me as being a high point of bridge-building in the sixteenth century. To fast forward to contemporary connections, Barnett Newman was profoundly stimulated by Grünewald's masterpieces, which provided confirmation for his desire to employ the Christian narrative in his *Stations of the Cross* series.[3] Newman said that Grünewald's Crucifixion is maybe the greatest painting in Europe. He was most intrigued by Grünewald's imagination that gave him the ability to identify with the agony of patients and turn the Christ figure into a syphilitic.[4]

The Isenheim Altarpiece is composed of panels commissioned to be part of a healing program for patients with blood and skin disorders as well as epilepsy.[5] One panel features St. Anthony as the protagonist. He screams with pain as he is tormented by demonic, weird creatures and a giant parrot. No wonder *Temptation of Saint Anthony* was only shown once a year.[6] Yet suffering patients could identify with him.

1. Stokstad, *Art History*, 731.
2. Cork, *The Healing Presence of Art*, 75.
3. Ibid., 85.
4. Ibid.
5. Ibid., 75.
6. Ibid., 76–79.

Images of Light

There are panels with lighter touches. *Virgin and Child with Angelic Concert* is festive, even suggesting celebration of the birth of the Christ child.[7] *Saint Anthony with Saint Paul the Hermit* depicts the two men having a pleasant conversation. A deer rests between them.[8] These happy images suggest to me that life is not all pain and suffering. Would people at the time find consolation in them? I do not know. I do know that sometimes people, including me, need encouragement to embrace good cheer.

The Crucifixion is the middle section. The mendicant order that commissioned it hoped that it would aid healing.[9] Christ on the cross has the same skin diseases as many of the patients. The painting makes it clear that Christ knew how harrowing it was to suffer maladies of the flesh.[10] Rather than confirming the patients' despair, looking at the *Crucifixion* could have released patients from shame and given them spiritual well being.[11]

Beyond the agony, Grünewald painted the *Resurrection* on a side panel of the altarpiece. In this painting blue and golden yellow have symbolic import. Under the resurrected Jesus' feet there is a cloth painted in what today we name cobalt and ultramarine and Russian blue. These blues are very clear and not at all muddy. Blue, especially the pure hues in *Resurrection* suggest to me the habitation of God because the blue reminds me of Exodus 24:9–10. In these verses the elders of Israel went up a mountain and saw the God of Israel. Under his feet there was something like a pavement of sapphire stones, like the very heaven for clearness.

7. Ibid., 79.
8. Ibid.
9. Ibid., 74.
10. Ibid., 81.
11. Ibid., 82.

Light of Resurrection

In *Resurrection* Jesus is backlit by a glowing yellow and orange sun that infuses Jesus' healed body. The glow of the sun is even more brilliant than what artists call glazed light. "The light created by Grünewald's brilliant, deep-glazed surface is too dense to conform to the traditional definition of a glaze—a thin film of transparent paint placed over an opaque, lighter color. Grünewald's enamel-like surfaces emanate a dense color-light unlike any other . . . the blinding light engulfing the Christ figure melts his face and transforms it into pure light. Seen at a distance, the glow spreads out to cover the whole surface . . . the feeling of the color-light is so fresh that one feels as if the painter has just recently applied the last brushstroke."[12] Jesus' arms are reaching up to God. Look at his hands. This resurrection is definitely a thumbs-up moment! Jesus lived to God's glory during his life and Jesus the Christ is glorified in the resurrected life and through his on-going teachings that light the world. Cork's most important sentence about this panel is: "The most astounding aspect of this panel lies in its light, blinding enough to oust any doubts about the plausibility of a resurrection."[13] Therefore this picture offered comfort and consolation at the time it was painted. Surely the circle of glorious golden Resurrection light has symbolically spoken to people throughout the centuries.

In the picture *The Virgin and Child with St. George and St. Anthony Abbott,* by Antonio Pisanello, who was a distinguished painter in the early Italian Renaissance, the infant Jesus and Mary are also depicted in a nebulous globe of light with beautiful rays of yellow and blue. Pulsating energy radiates as if to anticipate the Holy Spirit filled with light swirling throughout the world. Neither of the saints looks up at the virgin and child. The artist might have

12. Chaet, *An Artist's Notebook,* 226.
13. Cork, *The Healing Presence of Art,* 82.

simply been more interested in the saints' hats and metal armor that he did so well in his work with metals. Alternatively perhaps in the mindset of their day the saints lack a theological aesthetic in which beauty matters. Or perhaps do not want to look up because they understand that their vision is an inner glimpse of divine light and do not want to imply a literal Marian sighting. Mary is lovely in white with a touch of blue. Her headpiece is especially attractive with ruffled folds. Jesus is wrapped in a yellow blanket that suggests the glorious light that he is. Viewed together the golden-yellow circles in Grünewald's *Resurrection* and in Pisanello's *The Virgin and Child with St. George and St. Anthony Abbott* connect the resurrection and birth of Jesus. The cycle of Jesus' life and ours is symbolized, or so it seems to me, in a circle of golden light.

Vincenzo Catena painted *The Supper at Emmaus*. He was an Italian painter of the Renaissance Venetian School. According to Luke 24 two disciples walked with the resurrected Jesus towards Emmaus. They invited Jesus to remain with them although they did not know him. Luke tells us that after Jesus blessed and broke the bread the two disciples who were with him recognized him (24:30–31). In the painting, *The Supper at Emmaus*, Jesus after his resurrection but not yet ascended to God breaks bread with his disciples. The tablecloth is a glowing yellow that matches the panel behind Jesus. The deep blue-green of Jesus's outer robe conveys liveliness and depth. The whole room radiates warmth and love extending to even a pet under the table. In class we wondered if the animal is a dog or a cat. Upon further thought we all wanted it to be a lamb as a symbol of Christ but saw claws and not hooves. An art teacher researched further. She e-mailed me: "I looked up some information about dog symbolism in European renaissance art and found that the dog under the table was indeed a

Light of Resurrection

symbol often used to connote trust and loyalty. The painting of *The Supper at Emmaus* by Titian, depicts a dog which is clearly a dog, some kind of spaniel. So I assume that the 'critter' under Catena's table is also a dog." Color, light, and faithfulness matter in this painting and in the lives of hopeful men and women.

Blue and yellow are important in *Pietà*. In summary of Erickson's observations and her use of primary sources in letters to van Gogh from his brother Theo, there is symbolic use of color in *Pietà* Instead of a halo, intense yellow light conveys the mystical quality of the dying Jesus. Mary's robe is painted in various shades of blue from light indigo to darkest royal that contrasts with the luminous glow of light on her face and hands. Deep blue was van Gogh's symbol of infinity.

In *Pietà* and *The Raising of Lazarus,* van Gogh replaced Christ's face with his own face.[14] Erickson goes on to say that he believed that temporal existence is a time of trial and pain with the ultimate hope of deliverance. In this personalized portrait of devout Mary and suffering Christ, Mary stands by Jesus' side embracing the Christ figure. Both Mary and Jesus are bathed in golden light streaming from the sun. The yellow morning light foreshadows Christ's resurrection and the regeneration van Gogh hoped to find for himself.[15]

Van Gogh did not worship the sun but the sun is important in his work. "More likely, van Gogh simply used the sun to represent Christ, as others had done in western art since the third century."[16] The lavish use of yellow represents the divine presence, the resurrection, love of God

14. Erickson, *At Eternity's Gate*, 7.
15. Ibid., 158–159.
16. Ibid., 156.

and light from above.[17] The sun is a tribute to Christ.[18] He based his work on Rembrandt's etchings. Van Gogh wrote to his brother Theo. "The etchings you sent me are very beautiful."[19] Van Gogh depicts Lazarus using his own face and a bit of red hair like his own. Lazarus is pale but warming up as he comes back to life. Mary and Martha are there, dressed in green and yellow that connotes spring renewal. Mountains in the distance are light greenish blue. The sun shines on Lazarus and warms him in body and soul. Embracing the happiness of sunshine yellow with the implication of ultimate restoration is not the answer to everything. Yet it is a start. So when you feel sad, take a walk in the sunlight and soak up the warmth as a gift of nature and of grace.

Blue as symbol of infinity converges with my story in which blue matters. As I wrote in the introduction blue was important to me as a three year old. My mother was dying from leukemia. Light filtered through cobalt vases on the windowsill and comforted me. Therefore intense blue in art does represent an aspect of my experience and continues to offer consolation often in the most surprising ways as you will see in the following story. This story about blue is based on a story published in my book *Protestant Pulse: Heart Hopes for God*.

The Story of the Indigo Buntings

WELCOME INTO ETERNAL LIFE is a huge hint that there is a loving God. This story suggests that there is heavenly life for people who do not go to church and are not

17. Ibid., 155.
18. Ibid., 156.
19. Uhde, *Passages from Van Gogh's Letters*, 10.

explicitly Christian. Lester, who was the best man at our wedding, asked if the following poem is true. Yes, it is.

Indigo Buntings

> Two weeks before Eleanor Parsons died
> I asked her for a sign from the Beyond
> Specifying two indigo buntings
> Loveliest birds, pure notes of heaven's song.
> Two birds don't have to be in the same place.
> Just one would seem like a coincidence.
> Double sightings would make a stronger case.
> Confirm God's wide welcome, love's deepest sense.
> Before the memorial service day
> A blessed sympathy note came in the mail
> An indigo bunting. "Thank you." I prayed.
> Bunting also on the back, my spirit sailed.
> Proof or temporal ambiguity
> Creating room for beauty's mystery?

Ellie, short for Eleanor, brought me up from the age of four after my first mother died. Her sister, Charlotte Hope (known as Hopie), who was egged on by her fundamentalist friend, told Ellie they were worried that she would not go to heaven because she was not a church member. Ellie did not know that they insisted that I get a chaplain to have her join a church, when Ellie was nearly on her deathbed. Although Ellie would not have put it this way, her sister's concern gave her a bit of an existential crisis, which only assurance of a place in heaven could neatly address. Stanley M. Harrison in his introduction to *The Self as Agent* by John Macmurray discusses Macmurray's understanding of ultimate reality and authentic religion that came early in his career. Drawing from Macmurray's essay, "Objectivity in Religion" (1927), Harrison observes that desire for personal dimensions to ultimate reality is the context for Macmurray's philosophical search for reality. Harrison says that Macmurray's central insight is simply stated. Summarizing Macmurray, Harrison wrote, "The concern that people naturally have about the character of ultimate reality is rooted in the desire that ultimate reality be personal. If ultimate reality, God, isn't personal, then our deepest concern as persons, symbolized by death, which threatens absolutely our existence in a personal world, can't finally be resolved."[20]

I supported Ellie and after her death put together an almost secular service. I remember how angry she was when as a teenager I wanted to join the Congregational Church and told me that I was just repeating things I had been told. That was not true. No one grows up or learns anything in a vacuum, but I have always thought for myself. Because my beliefs have not always been respected, I know how important it is to respect the beliefs of other people. An explicitly Christian service would not have been reflective of Ellie and even worse a sign of vindictiveness. Yet telling the story of the indigo bunting that Ellie would have loved testified to God's broad love.

I do think that a basic belief in Christianity is that people can change. I do not know if Ellie changed her mind about religion. Ellie did change her ideas about me and no longer saw me as the shame of our family because I am clumsy but as costar with Rosemary. Rosemary is my younger sister of heart and hearth. We were raised together after my first mother died. Rosemary is a Rockport harbormaster and also serves as an EMT. She is often featured in the local paper when she rescues people on land and sea.

Gay Williams presided at the memorial service. She was a member of the First Congregational Church of

---

20. Macmurray, *The Self as Agent*, xi.

Light of Resurrection

Verona, New Jersey, when Ernie was the minister there. She moved to Massachusetts and after semi-retirement became a hospital chaplain. Without knowing that Ellie was my second mother, Gay visited her in the Addison Gilbert Hospital in Gloucester, Masachusetts. Ellie had a slight stroke and could not remember my last name. Yet she told Gay that she had two daughters, Rosemary and Sharon, who are very different but both very nice. "Rosemary is a harbormaster and Sharon is a poet," she said. Ellie came to consider Gay a third daughter so Gay also known as GG was the perfect person to conduct Ellie's service. One of Ellie's friends told me the service was the one Ellie would have wanted.

As the poem states, I asked Ellie for a sign and told her that if she sent me two indigo buntings after she died, I would write a poem about it and send a copy to Aunt Hope and her friend. This request was a tall order. I have only seen two indigo buntings in my life. The first time I was eleven and spotted one in the backyard of our home in Pigeon Cove, which is the north village of Rockport. Ellie asked me how I knew the name of the bird. There was a tiny indigo bunting on the bottom of the fifth grade reader from the previous year. The second spotting was in 1969 on the edge of the parking lot in New Hampshire where people renewed their drivers' licenses.

Two indigo buntings came to me not as real birds but as photographs on a sympathy card from Betty and John, who live in Pigeon Cove. Betty told me that there were different birds in the box of cards, and she quickly picked one. Aunt Hopie was relieved. A few days after the service, I found a card from my friend Ann that I had saved. The flock of buntings grew. When I told this story to my friend, Judy, she sent me a card with two indigo buntings.

Buntings as symbol took flight. While sorting through Ellie's books, Rosemary found a book entitled, *The Indigo*

Images of Light

Bunting: A Memoir of Edna St. Vincent Millay by Vincent Sheean. In the chapter with the same name as the book, the author shared some of Millay's last words that help me deal with grief by rejoicing in the color blue of many birds and believing in the joy of a perfect day. Therefore blue comforted me when my first mother died and also when my second mother died. Sheean wrote that Millay's sister Norma found Millay's notebooks with parts of a sonnet and then words marked "another poem." I quote the couplets from the unfinished sonnet.

> Never before, perhaps, was such a sight—
> Only one sky (my breath!) and all that blue—
> Lapis, and Sèvres, and borage—every hue
> Of blue-jay—indigo bunting—bluebird's flight.[21]

The words marked "another poem" help me know that sometimes writers can write something that will matter even at the end of life and also trust that some days require grieving but not all. Father James F. Keenan's defined charity in his article "Charity, the Mother of the Virtues": "Charity is like a mother, guiding us lovingly but firmly to pursue what we love."[22] Millay's words encourage me to keep writing poetry, which is the work I love. Millay's notes for another poem help me with grief.

> I will control myself, or go inside.
> I will not flaw perfection with my grief.
> Handsome, this day: no matter who has died.[23]

Ellie, who was not comfortable with my interest in religion until the last year of her life, was not the person I ever thought would help me address a theological problem. However, receiving the indigo buntings on the card is data

---

21. Sheean, *The Indigo Bunting*, 31.
22. Keenan, "Charity, the Mother of the Virtues," 42.
23. Sheean, *The Indigo Bunting*, 32.

Light of Resurrection

to anecdotally support the existence of God and eternal life. Macmurray said that there is both an atheistic and theistic wing to existentialism. In his view the theistic alternative issues forth in the hope of an ultimate unity of persons in fellowship, which gives meaning to human efforts.[24] The story of the indigo buntings points to a wide fellowship in eternal life.

When the sky is purest blue and the world is lit by golden sunlight, there are vistas of beauty. As we ascend the mountains of our lives into eternity, embracing beauty is triumph.

QUESTIONS

1. Have you experienced vistas of beauty on your journey?
2. Is belief in life after death a necessary part of your faith? Why? Or why not?
3. Does pursuing what you love make you feel more at home in this world or give you a sense of purpose?
4. What do you think is the goal of your life?
5. What do you think is the end or fulfillment of faith?

---

24. Macmurray, *The Self As Agent*, 222.

Prayers

BECAUSE THIS BOOK IS for both Christian and Humanist readers, I wrote prayers that are theistic and statements that are humanistic. My hope is that these prayers and statements will be bridge-building between people of different perspectives.

CHAPTER 1

Gracious God,

As we look up imagining the Star of Bethlehem, we lift our hopes to you. By naming our desires, hopefulness rises from deep interior places of courage that give transcendent strength to strive for all that is good, and true, and beautiful. Amen.

Speaking from core values:

Imagining the Star of Bethlehem, we name our hopes and lift them to community. In community we find transcendent strength to find the good, the true, and the beautiful. So be it.

CHAPTER 2

Sustainer God,

Casting our bread upon the waters, ripples expand wider and wider. Good News, victory shouts of light;

Images of Light

reflect your inclusive love, dear Christ. Light of the world; illuminate our lives as individuals and as covenanted communities. Bread of Life, nourish us and help us share the sustenance. Amen.

Speaking from core values:

Casting our bread upon the waters, ripples of caring expand wider and wider. Inclusive love extends circles of caring. Victory shouts of light winning out over darkness sound in the foreground. So be it.

Chapter 3

Father-Mother God,

Please shine your pure light on our paths to wholeness and maturity of love. Help us to actualize Jesus's teachings and ethics of forgiveness in our on-going journeys. We strive to give a little light to those whose lives are darkened by despair and graciously accept gifts of kindness from others. Amen.

Speaking from core values:

In community we affirm our core-value of forgiveness as we journey together to a better world. We strive to give a little light to those whose lives are darkened by despair and graciously accept gifts of kindness from others. So be it.

Chapter 4

Compassionate God,

Empty our minds of needless preoccupation. Fill our hearts with compassion to see wounded people who walk on paths we also tread. Abide with us on our road to truest

Prayers

worship be it in our faith communities or on the highway of life. Amen.

Speaking from core values:

Emptying our minds of needless preoccupations we seek to fill our hearts with compassion to see wounded people on the paths we also tread. We make ourselves right with the universe with gifts of caring and welcome to wounded men and women and children. In community we affirm the worth of all people. So be it.

CHAPTER 5

Creator God,

May blue sky rushing towards us through green leaves be for us a symbol of the healing powers of holy rest in beauty and in light. Made in your image, priestly God, who established the rhythms of work and rest at the beginning of creation, we embrace the gift of rest in letting go, putting ourselves into your hands, and trusting in the ultimate purposefulness of the universe. Amen.

Speaking from core values:

May blue sky rushing toward us through green leaves give moments of healing and rest, wonder, and inner peace. So be it.

CHAPTER 6

In an attitude of prayer and speaking from determination:

Two words for theists and humanists to repeat three times.

Take courage. Take courage. Take courage.

Images of Light

CHAPTER 7

Transforming God,
   We hope that our efforts to be truth speakers and seekers of freedom for ourselves and for others will dissolve into you and into greatest goodwill at loose in the world. Grant us mystical moments of closeness with you in nature's sacramental beauty and in sacrament of bread and wine, in life and in literature, in art and in action. Amen.

Speaking from core values:

May our individual efforts at being truth speakers and freedom seekers meld into our ongoing life as an assembly of caring people and spread throughout the world. We seek inspiration from nature, beauty, art, literature, and the lives of other people. So be it.

CHAPTER 8

God of Easter, God of Joy,
   We give thanks for all that lifts the human heart: Resurrection, colors, light, days of sunshine, new beginnings, and vistas of beauty, family fellowship, and caring people. Amen.

Speaking from core values:

In community we rejoice in all that lifts the human spirit. Colors, light, days of sunshine, new beginnings, vistas of beauty, family fellowship, human love, and caring people. So be it.

Conclusion as Contraries

"The light needs the darkness to be articulate."
Laurence Whistler
Artist, poet, glass engraver
Father of Simon Whistler, glass engraver

EMBRACE GLIMPSES OF LIGHT that glow in darkness. Trust that darkness is symbolic of evil only when it hides light rather than serving as contrast to make light visible. Darkness is the cradle, which carries the light that brightens paths of ascent to trust in triumph. Darkness expresses hidden mystery in depths of ebony, sepia, brown, purple and deepest indigo blue. There would be no light without the dark. Dark and light together create radiance that streams in glory.

The shades of night and the colors of day were formed at creation and reflect the Creator of enlightenment and of mystery. For black is the color of the world's children with deepest hue, of a big, sleek dog, of Bible covers, of richest soils, of flowing pens, of rest in a period at the end of a sentence . . . of shingled roofs that shelter, of a beautiful night that makes the stars sparkle. The shimmering stars in their beauty inspire hopes that we, too, will shine and triumph to the glory of God and of humanity standing on tiptoe.

Images of Light

Radiance

> Crescent moon and morning star
> together shine in inky dark.
> "For darkness is as light with thee."
> The psalmist speaks in poetry.
>
> Together shine in inky dark,
> evening and morning merge as one.
> The psalmist speaks in poetry.
> Transcendence and time intertwine.
>
> Morning and evening merge as one.
> "For darkness is as light with thee."
> Transcendence and time intertwine
> crescent moon and morning star.

Appendix

Ella's Gift

A Christmas Eve Story of Light

SHORT, GRAYING HAIR FRAMED Ella's face. On the plump side, she favored black polyester pants with flowered tunic blouses, wearing them year-round. Heavy wool socks were her only concession to winter.

Ella looked through her kitchen window trimmed with red checkered curtains. Two weeks before Christmas, snow was already a foot deep in the fields. Yellow sky backlit Fred and Cora's farmhouse across the street. Once when Ella brought her elderly neighbors coffeecake, she overheard them, "Look," said Cora, "at those rosy peaches . . . one for you and one for me."

Ella did not have a pleasant marriage like Cora and Fred. Yet she made the most out of her life through her work as a deaconess of the Pilgrim Congregational Church of Wallville, New Hampshire.

Husband, Paul, like his father before him, sometimes drank too much. Paul's dad found the long Canadian winters depressing. He withdrew to the tavern. Paul's happiest childhood memories were evenings carving by the fireplace. His mother and sisters knitting fancy mittens were good company. As a teenager, Paul found solace by visiting Benedictine brothers at a nearby monastery. Community openness to God strengthened his faith, although he started to define personal freedom as detachment from home. Old patterns continued. Paul still wanted to remain aloof while keeping a woman waiting. On the weekends he lived upstairs where his unhappiness wouldn't bother anyone. During the week he literally and metaphorically stayed on the straight and narrow while he trucked a mountain highway.

Both girls were married. Ella felt closest to their youngest daughter, Sarah. She managed a gift shop and often sent knickknacks to her mother. Rose, a high school English teacher, disliked clutter. She preferred plain Shaker furniture and winter days when snow simplified the landscape.

The similarities between Rose and the young minister's wife crossed Ella's mind. She was not sure that Pastor Pete and Heather would like her decorating ideas. Pete, like his wife, needed order. One day when stopping by Pastor Pete's office, Ella noticed a reproduction of a Mondrian painting of black lines with blue and yellow squares. Ella thought, "I have those same colors in my glass vases. Sunlight dances in them."

A cliché passed through Ella's mind. "Nothing ventured; nothing gained." In the afternoon she dropped by the parsonage. Heather was home with three-year-old Christopher. Pete was visiting parishioners. Heather apologized for toys all over the living room. Ella said, "Not to worry. Your home looks more lived in now." Heather relaxed in the warmth of Ella's acceptance.

Ella told Heather that she found a crèche set while cleaning the basement of the local bank, which was her way of making a little extra money to buy Christmas presents. She asked if she might borrow it. The bank president, Mr. Babis, who was tired of storing the set, said, "Might as well

Ella's Gift

get some use out of it." He told Ella that his brother, Stephen, gave him the set when his Greek Orthodox Church near Boston bought a new one. "Would you like the 4H animals, too?"

Pete returned. Ella repeated her story. Pete looked to Heather for advice. "A crèche set is a beautiful addition to Christmas," said Heather imagining small, olive-wood figures. "Just remember," interjected Pete, "the family who gave the communion table asked that decorations never be placed on it."

"My kitty is praying," said Christopher. Sid, short for Siddhartha, was part Siamese with curly whiskers. He folded his paws under his body, appearing to meditate.

Heather explained to Ella. "I upset Mrs. Jones by calling Sid a Zen Buddhist cat. She didn't want to hear about anything she considers pagan."

Ella replied, "My sister gave me a Buddha she found at a garage sale. Any religion with that much peace must be good. Mrs. Jones is just scared."

Pleased with permission to decorate, Ella left the parsonage thinking how she would honor the Prince of Peace. "I must wait until the last minute so as not to spoil the surprise. Perhaps Paul will help."

When Paul came home, Ella shared her plans over coffee. Paul got up from the table saying, "I'll be right back." He climbed the stairs, passed his hideaway, lowered the fold-up ladder and entered the dark hole into the attic. There under the eves was the old trunk. Paul gingerly lifted the covers. He found the ornate crucifix he carved as a boy. Morning glories climbed to Christ and gently enfolded him. Paul almost smiled as if by feeling the agony of the crucified Jesus, he embraced and let go of his own pain. His heart felt warm. Although he would not have put it this way, he had a Wesleyan moment. Paul carried his gift downstairs and handed his offering to Ella. Tears came to her eyes. "Thank

Images of Light

you." Ella thought, "He really listened when I explained my desire to make the story of God's love more visible."

On Christmas Eve, Heather and Pete were behind. Heather had presents to wrap. Pete cut himself shaving. Plus, John, a middle-aged man with a beard, phoned to suggest that since legends say animals speak on Christmas Eve, Pete might mention animal rights in his meditation.

Pete had come to value John's child-like innocence that reminded him of Christopher and his toy animals. The kind ladies of the Women's Fellowship were aghast at Christopher's black and white mobile, even with Heather's explanation that these colors help young eyes focus. To add a soft touch, they gave a stuffed animal shower in the tradition of Noah's ark, with two of each animal. Christopher, like John, loved bears and bunnies, squirrels and skunks.

Pilgrim Congregational was a simple meetinghouse. A plain, gold cross on red velvet hung over the altar. In keeping with the Puritan tradition, the windows were clear glass that let in views of the outside and other church steeples. There was one small stained glass window in the upstairs loft in the back of the church that was composed of geometric shapes like the Mondrian print in the pastor's study. Light shone through red, blue, and yellow glass and sometimes on the sunniest of days cast colored light onto the plain sanctuary walls. On Christmas Eve, red poinsettia plants were always placed in the chancel and on the windowsills of the clear glass windows. This year the florist put them wherever he could find room. Ella had filled every spot in the church, except for the communion table, to the glory of God.

The whole nativity scene and half the town of Bethlehem were there in life-size plywood figures. Wise men and camels walked down one aisle; shepherds and their flocks processed the other. Angels with tinsel halos waltzed down

Ella's Gift

the center aisle. A mother pig nursing three piglets rested between the pulpit and the first pew.

The crèche was in the chancel. Ella did not find a star and gave up trying to fashion a five-pointed one. She made a Star of David that shone over the holy family with a blessed reminder of Jesus' family heritage. The holy child, sitting up in the manger, had an adult face like Christ in a Greek Orthodox Pantocrator. Mary looked lovely. The white paint on her head covering had chipped. So Ella covered Mary's head with a pure, white, silk scarf that Rose's friend, Ramie, had given Ella. The soft scarf visually echoed the tenderness on Mary's face. Ella was proud of Rose for having friends from many faith traditions. Ramie, a devout Muslim, was pleased that her name tied her to her traditions yet sounded so American like Angie, Amy or Jodie. Ella paused and thought, "Ramie's gentleness is a spring breeze."

Ella wanted frankincense but had forgotten to order some from her religious notions catalog. Her friend, Barbara, shared her incense, a gift from her daughter-in-law, with Ella, who was good at "making do." Hindu incense simmered in a crock-pot behind the wise men. Ella placed the crucifix next to the sign posting the hymns.

Mrs. Tully, the choir director, entered the church and gasped. The cherub angel choir would just have to walk the best they could. One active boy bumped into a little girl who lost her halo. A dairy farmer's son said, "See the brown cow looking at Jesus!"

Processing down the aisle, Pete thought, "My meditation on the simplicity of Christmas will not do." He felt a rising flush of anger and then in a twinkling he realized that the sanctuary was enchanting, like Christopher's room full of toy animals. Ella's decorating reflected divine playfulness in a peaceable kingdom. Images of peace and play, symbols and scent formed a collage in his mind.

Images of Light

The congregation listened to readings and sang carols. Pete walked to Joseph's side. "We are gathered here as people together," on Noah's ark crossed his mind, but he said, "Like pilgrims on the Mayflower. For we are all pilgrims on the earth we share. Our faith journeys may intersect as we meet at the cross or the crossroads."

Sid, the parsonage cat, wandered into the sanctuary. He leaped upon the communion table, as cats will do, and folded his paws in meditative position. Pete glanced at him and went on. "Consider the symbols here. There is a Roman Catholic crucifix, a Byzantine Jesus, a Star of David and incense from I know not where. I do know that God touches us through all our senses. Love is born when we wish all people and creatures well. Let us join together in a circle with our candles. We are all bearers of holy light. As the angels of the first Christmas sang, 'Peace on earth, good will . . .'"

Print Sources for Images

BY USING YOUR FAVORITE search engine you can find many of the paintings discussed in this book. The following list includes the title of the painting, the artist, the title of the book in which I found the painting, and the author of the book. For more details about the books, please see the bibliography.

Nuit de Noel
Henri Matisse
The Cut-outs of Henri Matisse, page 80
John Elderfield

Simeon's Song of Praise
Aert de Gelder
Sister Wendy's 1000 Masterpieces, page 165
Sister Wendy Beckett

The Return of the Prodigal Son
Rembrandt van Rijn
The Return of the Prodigal Son: A Story of Homecoming, cover painting
Henri J. M. Nouwen

The Good Samaritan (after Delacroix)
Vincent van Gogh
At Eternity's Gate: The Spiritual Vision of Vincent van Gogh, color plate 8
Kathleen Powers Erickson

Images of Light

> *Tree of Life,* Nave and Apse
> Henri Matisse
> *The Cut-outs of Henri Matisse,* pages 70–71
> John Elderfield
>
> *Christ Before the High Priest*
> Gerrit van Honthorst
> *Sister Wendy's* 1000 *Masterpieces,* page 214
> Sister Wendy Beckett
>
> *Sailing Boats*
> Lyonel Feininger
> *Sister Wendy's* 1000 *Masterpieces,* page 151
> Sister Wendy Beckett
>
> *The Glorious Victory of the Sloop "Maria"*
> Lyonel Feininger
> *The Visual Arts As Human Experience,* plate 16
> Donald L. Weismann
>
> *Resurrection*
> Mattthias Grünewald
> *Sister Wendy's* 1000 *Masterpieces,* page 195
> Sister Wendy Beckett
>
> *The Virgin and Child with St. George and St. Anthony Abbott*
> Antonio Pisano Pisanello
> *Sister Wendy's* 1000 *Masterpieces,* page 362
> Sister Wendy Beckett
>
> *The Supper at Emmaus*
> Vincenzo Catena
> *The Art Book,* page 88

Print Sources for Images

Pietà (After Delacroix)
Vincent van Gogh
At Eternity's Gate: The Spiritual Vision of Vincent van Gogh,
color plate 6
Kathleen Powers Erickson

The Raising of Lazarus (after Rembrandt)
Vincent van Gogh
At Eternity's Gate: The Spiritual Vision of Vincent van Gogh,
color plate 7
Kathleen Powers Erickson

Bibliography

Adams, Doug. "Changing Perceptions of Jesus' Parables through Art History: Polyvalency in Paint." In *Reluctant Partners: Art and Religion in Dialogue*, 68–87. New York: The Gallery at the American Bible Society, 2004.

Apostolos-Cappadona, Diane, editor. *Art, Creativity, and the Sacred: An Anthology in Religion and Art*. New York: Crossroad, 1984.

Beckett, Sister Wendy, and Patricia Wright. *Sister Wendy's 1000 Masterpieces*. New York: DK, 1999.

Chace, Sharon R. *Protestant Pulse: Heart Hopes for God*. Eugene, OR: Resource Publications, 2009.

Chaet, Bernard. *An Artist's Notebook: Techniques and Materials*. New York: Holt, Rinehart and Winston, 1979.

Cook, Harry T. *Long Live Salvation By Works: A Humanist Manifesto*, Salem, OR: Polebridge, 2012.

———. *Resonance: Biblical Texts Speaking to 21st Century Inquirers*. Salem, OR: Polebridge, 2011.

Cork, Richard. *The Healing Presence of Art: A History of Western Art in Hospitals*. New Haven, CT: Yale University Press, 2012.

Drury, John. *Painting the Word: Christian Pictures and their Meanings*. New Haven, CT: Yale University Press, 1999.

Durham, John I. *The Biblical Rembrandt: Human Painter in a Landscape of Faith*. Macon, GA: Mercer University Press, 2004.

Elderfield, John. *The Cut-outs of Henri Matisse*. New York: Braziller, 1978.

Erickson, Kathleen Powers. *At Eternity's Gate: The Spiritual Vision of Vincent van Gogh*. Grand Rapids: Eerdmans, 1998.

Fourcade, Yvonne. "Drawing with Scissors." *Reader's Digest* 115:691 (November 1979) 158–64.

Ganss, George E. *The Spiritual Exercises of Saint Ignatius: A Translation and Commentary*. Chicago: Loyola University Press, 1992.

Goldwater, Robert and Marco Treves, eds. *Artists On Art from the XIV to the XX Century*. New York: Pantheon, 1945.

González-Andrieu, Cecilia. *Bridge to Wonder: Art as a Gospel of Beauty*. Waco, TX: Baylor University Press, 2012.

Bibliography

Harrington, Daniel J. *Interpreting the New Testament: A Practical Guide.* Collegeville, MN: Liturgical Press, 1990.

———. *Why Do We Hope? Images in the Psalms.* Collegeville, MN: Liturgical Press, 2008.

Hazelton, Roger. *A Theological Approach to Art.* Nashville: Abingdon, 1967.

Heller, Ena Giurescu, ed. *Reluctant Partners: Art and Religion in Dialogue.* New York: The Gallery at the American Bible Society, 2004.

Hyman, Timothy. Review of *The Healing Presence in Art: A History of Western Art in Hospitals* by Richard Cork. *Times Literary Suppliment* (2012) 11.

Irwin, Eleanor. *Colour Terms in Greek Poetry.* Toronto: Hakkert, 1974.

Janson, H. W. *History of Art.* New York: Harry N. Abrams, Inc. 1963.

Keenan, James F. "Charity, the Mother of the Virtues." *Church* 10:4 (1994) 41–42.

Macmurray, John. *The Self As Agent.* Amherst, NY: Humanity, 1957.

Miles, Margaret R. *Image as Insight: Visual Understanding in Western Christianity and Secular Culture.* Eugene, OR: Wipf & Stock, 1985.

Nouwen, Henri J. M. *The Return of the Prodigal Son: A Story of Homecoming.* New York: Doubleday, 1992.

O'Roark, Mary Ann. "A Beautiful Place." *Guideposts* 56.1 (March 2001) 40–45.

Phaidon Press. *The Art Book.* London: Phaidon, 1994.

———. *Vincent van Gogh.* Vienna: Phaidon, 1936.

Reklau, Frederick. *Partners in Care: Medicine and Ministry Together.* Eugene, OR: Resource Publications, 2010.

Rockport Reporter, "Religious Art Is Anything that Knocks You for a Loop." *Gloucester Daily Times* 104:195 (August 19, 1964) 2.

Rodari, Florian. *Collage: Pasted, Cut, and Torn Papers.* Translated by Michael Taylor. New York: Rizzoli, 1988.

Sheean, Vincent. *The Indigo Bunting: A Memoir of Edna St. Vincent Millay.* New York: Schocken, 1951.

Stokstad, Marilyn. *Art History.* Revised Edition. New York: Abrams, 1999.

Swenson, Kristin. *Bible Babel: Making Sense of the Most Talked About Book of All Time.* New York: Harper, 2010.

Tillich, Paul. *Dynamics of Faith.* New York, Harper, 1957.

———. *The Shaking of the Foundations.* New York: Scribner's, 1948.

Uhde, Wilhelm. *Passages from Van Gogh's Letters.* Vienna: Phaidon, 1936

Bibliography

Waldron, Robert. "Still Life." *Boston College Magazine* 70.1 (Winter 2010) 46–49.

Watts, Greg. *Rembrandt*, Oxford, England: Lion Hudson, 2009.

Weismann, Donald L. *The Visual Arts As Human Experience*. Englewood Cliffs, NJ: Prentice-Hall, 1974.

Zerwick, Max, and Mary A. Grosvenor. *A Grammatical Analysis of the Greek New Testament—Unabridged*. Fourth Edition. Rome: Editrice Pontificio Istituto Biblico, 1993.